Care and

PRINCIPLES OF PASTORAL
COUNSELLING

Other Books on Care and Counselling

R. S. Lee

PRINCIPLES OF PASTORAL COUNSELLING

LONDON
SPCK

First published in the Library of Pastoral Care 1968
Reissued in the Care and Counselling Series 1978
SPCK
Holy Trinity Church
Marylebone Road
London NW1 4DU

Printed in Great Britain by
William Clowes & Sons, Limited
London, Beccles and Colchester

ISBN 0 281 03565 2

Contents

Preface

Pastoral counselling has sprung up in recent years in the effort to adapt psychoanalytic procedures to the solution of some of the common problems which are met in the pastoral work of the clergy. It has been largely an empirical venture, proceeding by rule of thumb, learning by experience. Nevertheless the great pioneers, whose work on the whole has proved outstandingly successful, began with an extensive knowledge of dynamic psychology. In trying to pass on their skills to a wider group of their fellow clergy they rightly lay much emphasis on the need for practical training as the only way to acquire the skills, and above all the attitudes, which mark the successful counsellor. The emphasis on work in clinics, with individuals and groups, has led to occasional under-valuation of the need for theoretical knowledge of the working of the human mind and of the reasons why practical training is necessary. It has also led to some confusion between the role of the counsellor and the psychotherapist.

This book is intended as a brief introduction to the principles on which pastoral counselling is based. It is not a manual of practice. Volumes dealing with specific kinds of problem in which pastoral counselling has proved valuable are listed on p. i. Because of the limits of space imposed on this volume there are glaring omissions, such as, for instance, discussion of the psychological factors which are at work in adolescence and senescence, and the change of balance in emotional drives occurring in middle age. Perhaps the greatest omission is any consideration of the problems which arise from the fact that the development of women follows a different line from that of men, to which this book is confined. For the ways in which feminine attitudes differ from masculine, readers are referred to the writer's *Your Growing Child and Religion* (Penguin Books) which ought to be read in conjunction with the present volume, since it gives a fuller picture of the stages of development on the way to maturity.

The general principles set out in the following pages apply in the counselling of both men and women. It is offered to all who may be involved in pastoral care of any kind in the hope that they may find a general treatment useful in guiding them to a deeper understanding of the problems they encounter in their work, of the role of the pastor in helping people in trouble and of the areas in which pastoral care can be effective.

I wish to thank Dr D. W. Winnicott and the Hogarth Press for permission to quote from him in Chapters 6 and 7 and in doing so to express my admiration for his enormous contribution to our knowledge of the dynamics and development of the human mind.

R. S. LEE

1

Pastoral Care and
Pastoral Counselling

There have always been great counsellors in the Church. The skills and the wisdom which made them outstanding among their brethren have come to them in the course of their work, not as a result of special training aimed to develop in them the competence they have possessed as "pastoral counsellors". It is not at all easy to determine how they became what they were, or are, but it is fair to assume that the qualities of character they manifest have much to do with it. Among these qualities the most significant seem to be humility, selflessness, sympathy for and patience with others giving them the ability to listen with understanding, and an unshakeable faith in the healing and renewing action of God, a faith which includes in it a deep love of our fellow men and respect for their freedom and independence.

That such men are comparatively rare would be generally admitted, but perhaps they are not as rare as the praise by Chaucer of the Parson in his "Canterbury Tales" and by Goldsmith of the Vicar of Auburn ("The Deserted Village") would seem to indicate. Nevertheless they are sufficiently rare to make it clear that the normal training given to carefully selected men and the practice of their vocation do not inevitably produce in the clergy these qualities which would be universally held to be desirable. The failure, in so far as there has been failure, has been highlighted in the last few decades by an increasing understanding of the emotional, social, and moral difficulties from which men and women suffer. To meet these there has sprung up a whole set of new professions, psychotherapists, social workers of many categories, guidance bureaux of various kinds, and groups like Alcoholics Anonymous. Most of these are given rigorous training for the specialized work they are called to do. Nevertheless, it has been found in the United States that it is still to the clergy that the largest number of people come to seek help with their personal problems. The same may be true of Britain, but the figures are not available. It is commonly asserted that there has been a great increase in the number of people suffering from mental breakdowns which partially or wholly incapacitate them from normal living, rendering them unable to adjust to society or to bear the responsibilities which are part of social relationships. There may be an increase, or it may be that we have become more aware of the personal disabilities such people suffer, or perhaps the pressures of modern life are so severe that disabilities which in previous generations have been latent or manifested only in minor forms have now been brought out into the open. Whatever the actual situation, the Churches have lagged behind in meeting the need and it is only in the last few years that widespread effort has begun to remedy the situation. Various schemes have been started to give clergy and ordinands training in the skills which seem necessary to help people suffering from the various disabilities, particularly, if we may anticipate at this point, those springing from inadequate emotional development, for this has been found to be the root cause even of most problems which at first sight appear to be of a moral, criminal, or even spiritual character.

For some years the United States has taken the lead in this new movement. Under the Council for Clinical Training a large number of centres were set up in which, under the direction of psychotherapists, chaplains, and social workers, clergy and ordinands are given training, largely of a practical character, in the methods and aims of clinical psychology. Considerable use has been made of these courses and it is now almost universal for ordinands in the (Anglican) Protestant Episcopal Church to undergo such training as part of their course in the various seminaries. And other denominations have all made considerable use of them or similar courses they have set up. In the last year or two, however, some rethinking about it has taken place. The value of such training has not been questioned. If anything there has been an increased sense of its importance. What has been called into question is the aim that lies behind it, and the results which the short courses (three months, six months, or even a year) can be expected to achieve.

In taking note of the shortcomings of the programme for clinical training we should set these against the great benefits it has brought—an enormous increase in general pastoral efficiency, understanding of the causes underlying personal failures, and a new and positive attitude towards them. These gains must not be sacrificed. We may even hope to improve on them if we take note of the weaknesses of the system. Opportunities of training are springing up all over Britain and we should be on the watch lest we fall into the same errors. There are two main ones. The first is that of attempting too much in the time available. The emphasis may be laid on "counselling" rather than on "pastoral". In the United States the office of counsellor is a long established one and almost every school, college, or university has at least one counsellor to whom students in any kind of difficulty are referred. It is true that many hold the post with a minimum of training, but in general a considerable knowledge of dynamic psychology and practical training in the techniques of counselling are regarded as essential to a successful counsellor. The work of counselling borders on and even overlaps that of the psychotherapist, and in many instances the counsellor is a trained psychotherapist. In the training of pastoral counsellors the trainees usually work with a psychotherapist and even where he is careful to point out the limits of their competence they begin to feel themselves incipient psychotherapists. The time required for membership of the American Institute of Psychoanalysis from the beginning of medical studies is fifteen years of rigorous work, so however assiduous a minister or seminarian may be in the few months of his clinical training he cannot hope to become a competent psychotherapist. Yet the evidence seems to show that many who go through the training assume that they have the competence to undertake therapeutic work. In so doing they are running the risk of doing harm to the unfortunates who come into their care. We need therefore to define the aims of training with greater precision, and make these clear not only to those who undergo training but also to those who are responsible for giving the training.

The second failure runs deeper but is not so obvious. It reveals itself in the approach to pastoral work displayed in many parish priests. They find that ordinary parochial work does not produce the quick results which they had hoped to achieve. They begin to think of themselves as failures, or they get bored with the daily routine of the work, endless committees, clubs, superficial contacts, and so on, and they try to get the results by plunging into counselling, which then becomes a substitute for pastoral care. They really place the emphasis on method, on technique, rather than on the deeper values which counselling demands to make it effective. And having failed as pastors, they fail also as counsellors.

The root cause of their failure is not inadequacy of method but that, because of the emphasis laid on this in their training (for technique is highly important), they conceive counselling to lie entirely in method. They have not been brought to a thoroughgoing integration of psychology and theology. Most important of all, their own fundamental inadequacies have not been brought to light and dealt with. Perhaps the need for the counsellors to be counselled is an independent matter, but it is a necessary step to reach the harmonious unity between their religious values and their psychological understanding, without which pastoral counselling will fail, or at best achieve uncertain results.

It is one thing to see this weakness in training for pastoral counselling, another to provide against it. Usually few of those undergoing training have sufficient knowledge of psychology, especially in its application to themselves, and fewer still can grasp that acceptance of the knowledge of man that has come through psychology makes inevitable an alteration in emphasis in religious teaching and in some aspects the modification or jettisoning of some commonly taught theological doctrines or religious attitudes. The leaders of religious thought, and especially those whose office or position in some measure commits them to current ortho- doxy, are as yet not seized with the necessity to come to terms with the findings of modern psychology. They are in many instances, we may even say now in most instances, ready to acknowledge the value of clinical training as a contribution to pastoral care, and to further it, but the challenge to doctrinal positions has not yet been squarely faced, except by a few writers.

These are matters which must be taken up in more detail in later chapters. At this point, however, we should consider whether or not pastoral counselling should be organized as a specialist ministry. Experience to date shows that consider- ably more training than has been available is needed to fit clergy for the work of counselling if it is to be carried out at the level of effectiveness which is attained by professional counsellors in other fields. Further, it seems clear that the work of counselling demands qualities of character, and abilities, which are not necessarily sought in the first place when the men are being selected as approved candidates for the ministry. It may be, though this is by no means certain, that the needed qualities and abilities will be developed in them by suitable training, but that training would need to be much more rigorous and far more extensive than is given at the present time. It has been suggested, in view of the difficulties in the way of giving all clergy this thoroughgoing training, that we should aim at a specialized ministry, perhaps non-parochial. A few men could be properly trained to be counsellors and other clergy could refer to them the people in need of psychological counselling. There is much that is attractive in this idea. Given the funds to cover the training and to carry out such a ministry it could be organized easily enough. It would, I think, be too heavy a burden to lay on men already involved in all the demands of a parochial ministry, so such expert counsellors would need to be freed from other responsibilities to devote all their time, or as much time as is demanded, to counselling work. Some big churches in populous city centres might carry such a man on their staff, as does, for instance, Trinity Church, Wall Street, New York, where one of the senior priests does nothing but counselling, apart from assisting in the services in the church. Another way would be to set up counselling centres, adequately staffed with psychologists as well as counsellors, in each city or diocese. These would have the advantage that they would make co-operation with other denominations possible. Or attached to some churches who could carry it there might be established counselling clinics with consultant psychiatrists sharing in the work. This is the model followed by Dr Leslie Weatherhead at the City Temple Clinic, London, and by Dr Vincent Peale at Marble Collegiate Church, Fifth Avenue, New York. At the latter place, however, the Foundation of Religion and Psychiatry has become largely independent and provides opportunities for research and training as well as being a place of counselling for those in need. Another mode of working is in the nature of a compromise but it has proved valuable where it can be organized. In this case a group of five or six clergy, usually of different denominations, who have had some training in counselling, meet regularly—once a week seems best—with a sympathetic psychiatrist, trained in psychotherapy, in what is really a case conference. They report the cases they are handling and discuss together what steps they have taken and hear the comments of the psychiatrist. Such meetings are useful both as training sessions and for the group therapeutic effect they have on the participants. The extent to which such centres and such groups can be organized depends not only on the heavy expenditure involved but also on the willingness of psychiatrists to give their services at what must always be a considerable cost to themselves. Whatever the form in which the specialist counselling ministry is organized, there should be at least one psychiatrist in support of it to advise where necessary and to whom the more difficult cases may be referred for treatment that is beyond the competence of the counsellor. If there is a psychiatrist in the background the pastoral counsellor is less likely to mistake his desire to help in a particular case for his ability to do so. Working with a psychiatrist enables him to recognize the limits of his competence, but it also reveals the ways in which he can give unlimited help which does not depend upon his professional and technical ability.

We may, then, accept that there is a strong case in favour of setting up a specialized ministry in one form or another and, as a corollary, of developing courses of training to equip men for this ministry, but this does not rule out the question of training for all clergy and social workers of the Church. Admitted that the full training cannot be given to all and that perhaps some are not suited to receive it, there still is need for some training to be given to all. Such training need not be considered as second class and inferior to the fuller training. It should be aimed to produce better pastors, not specialist pastoral counsellors. It is possible to be a good pastor without being a pastoral counsellor in the technical sense. Professor van den Berg, who used to teach "Practical Theology" in the Dutch Reformed Church at Utrecht and Rotterdam, once told me that he took his classes for a three year course in Pastoralia, and after that selected those who showed a bent for counselling and gave them a further two years of specialized training. This did not mean rejection of those who were not selected for the second course. He was simply differentiating between pastors and those whose special gifts fitted them to become counsellors. The first three years course was devoted to training pastors.

No parish priest (I hope I may be permitted for convenience sake to include under this term ministers in any Church working with a congregation) can evade pastoral responsibilities. He has many duties to perform as part of his office. He is called to proclaim the gospel by his preaching and teaching and to expound and interpret the scriptures. He has to educate both young and old in the doctrines and history of Christianity and of his own Church in particular, and this ought to include comparison with other Churches and faiths. It should also include exposition of the relevance of the Christian faith to the secular aspects of the contemporary world in its manifold complexity. He must lead his congregation in worship and minister the sacraments to them. In most of these duties, and in most of the churches, he is not merely the leader of the local congregation, but he is also the representative to it of the wider comprehensive Church which has trained and ordained him to its ministry. Even in Churches such as the Baptist or Congregational, this holds in practice, though not in theory. Hence in all these functions he is inevitably an authority figure, whether because of the specialized training he has had, in theology, for instance, or simply because of his office. But over and above that he has to be pastor to his congregation and to those beyond the inner circle of worshippers who from time to time turn to him for help in difficulty or who are at least formally committed to his ministry. He has to visit them to establish personal relations with them, to comfort them in trouble or sickness, to console them in bereavement, assist them in all their difficulties so far as he is able. He has to be their leader and their servant at all times. In all this work he has to knit them into a fellowship marked by mutual love, trust, and respect, a fellowship whose aim is not itself but devotion to the service of God and man.

It is obvious that in the course of his work the parish

priest will be called on to give pastoral counsel to individuals or to families among his people. For some problems he may find trained counsellors on whose assistance he can call, such as the Marriage Guidance Council or local government experts in various branches of social service. In some places there will be individual pastoral counsellors within convenient reach with adequate training to be rated as experts, or there may be pastoral clinics to help him out. These, however, are so few at present and generally so busy that the parish priest is compelled to undertake the counselling himself, for he must not turn away anyone who comes to him for help when there is no one else at hand to whom to refer him.

In the ideal state of affairs it may be advisable to have enough trained pastoral counsellors to cover every area. But only "may be". Further experience is needed to prove this and already there are signs that more effective help is potentially to be found within the local congregation, given the right leadership and training. Since it must be a long time in any case before a sufficient network of fully trained counsellors can be set up, the immediate need is for all clergy to be given some training to enable them to benefit from what has been learned from the development of pastoral counselling in recent years. What that training should be and upon what it is based will be discussed in the following chapters.

There is, however, one difficulty which should be made plain from the beginning, for it is so severe that it has led some people to say that it cannot be overcome and it therefore renders the parish priest incapable of being a pastoral counsellor in any significant sense. It has been found from much experience that the successful counsellor has to divest himself of authoritarianism, whether of an official or functional character, or as passing moral judgment on his client. He must not even be too ready with diagnostic suggestions. Since the parish priest has in many aspects of his work to appear as an authority, as we have seen, this is thought by some to debar him from the outset from becoming a good counsellor. We shall discuss this point in greater detail in later chapters. The difficulty is real enough but it is not insuperable. It does mean, however, that if the parish priest is to use the methods of counselling in his pastoral work he must arrive at a true reconciliation between the different roles he will be called on to play. He may become so skilled that he can completely divest himself of authoritarianism if counselling seems to be needed when help is sought for him. Better still, he may find that he can free himself in all his work from the authoritarian attitude, in which case he will probably find much greater success in his non-counselling work. At any rate these possibilities need to be considered.

If, then, we accept the possibility that the parish priest may be trained to use counselling methods satisfactorily in some aspects of his work, we can set out four groups of counsellors:

The untrained.   These may or may not be good counsellors. By reason of their natural gifts or as the result of training in other areas or of their mode of life, they may possess real pastoral ability. This cannot be taken for granted and experience seems to indicate that very few of the untrained reach this level.

Trained pastors.   Next to these can be set those who are trained in what I am calling "pastoral care". These will not be specialists in counselling except in rare instances and they will, by nature of their duties as parish priests, be called on to use counselling only occasionally. But their pastoral work should be based on counselling methods.

Pastoral counsellors.   These will be specialists who have been given a more thorough training and in most cases will either give most of their time to counselling or will do their counselling in separation from their other duties, in a clinic or counselling centre, for instance. Such pastoral counsellors will be the analogue of counsellors in other fields, but, as we shall see later, with one important difference.

Psychotherapists.   Finally, at the top of the scale we must put fully trained psychotherapists or psychiatrists, whose training is far longer and far more rigorous than that needed to equip counsellors. Their work cannot be called pastoral in the usual sense of the term. But they have to be included in the list not merely because it is desirable that pastoral counsellors should work in co-operation with psychotherapists, but because the methods of counselling are derived from the practice of psychotherapy and the knowledge of the dynamics of the human mind which has been gained through it.

2

The Unconscious in Counselling and Psychotherapy

In the previous chapter a distinction was drawn between pastoral care and pastoral counselling, a distinction analogous to that between medical general practitioners and consultant specialists. The parish priest is in the position of the general practitioner since he is required to deal with the whole range of parish work. He does not have the rigorous training necessary to the specialist pastoral counsellor. Nevertheless as in medicine so in pastoral work there are essential common principles in the training of both. The specialist simply has extra training in his particular field and since he confines himself to it gets much greater experience and therefore more skill in that field. But their basic training is the same.

In medicine the need for specialist training has long been recognized but it is only in comparatively recent times that the need and the value of such training for specialist work in counselling has come to be seen. It had to wait upon the development of psychoanalysis and other modern forms of psychotherapy which have brought new insights into the functioning of the mind and new methods to deal with problems of human development. These came from the effort to treat mental diseases by the methods of psychoanalysis, treatment which was without any religious aim whatsoever. But it is now clear that the principles of psychoanalysis have a wide application in pastoral work. This was recognized first in the field of pastoral counselling and then it was seen to be important in the more general field of pastoral care. As has already been said, the first efforts were directed towards training the clergy as counsellors, for it was assumed that they had a good training for general pastoral work, and it is only now that it has been realized that some of the methods devised for training in counselling apply to pastoral work as well. Throughout this book the need to distinguish between general pastoral care and specialist pastoral counselling will be maintained, recognizing that sometimes it will be impossible to draw a line of demarcation, but for convenience sake we may speak of training in counselling as applicable to both, because the emphasis will be on the new type of training that is required and the new attitudes which have to be fostered both in pastoral care and in counselling. This book is intended for the guidance of general pastors, some of whom may of course go on to become specialists; so where the term pastoral counsellor is used it refers to the work of the former unless the context makes it quite clear that the reference is to the specialist.

The new methods and the new attitudes derive from psychoanalysis. Psychoanalysis owes its origin and main development to the genius of Sigmund Freud. Sixty years ago only Freud and a bare handful of his disciples were following his ideas and methods. Today they and variant forms of them dominate the field of psychological medicine. Freud developed, expanded, modified his concepts considerably in the course of his life and any attempt to give a systematic exposition of his teachings has to take account of these changes and of the alteration of emphasis which they brought with them. No single one of his books does this.[1] Quite early on some of his disciples, notably Jung and Adler, put forward theories of human behaviour differing from those of Freud, and around them schools of thought and

---

[1] See, however, D. Stafford-Clark, *What Freud Really Said* (Penguin Books).

practice grew up and continue to develop. There have been many other variants on the basic Freudian ideas, and within the orthodox (if it may be so called) Freudian school there have been developments of thought reaching beyond the writings of Freud or at best only suggested by him as avenues to be explored.

This book is not the place to discuss the superiority of one school over the other. All we need to note is that in spite of their differences there is a broad area of agreement among them about the essential characteristics of the human mind. All are concerned with the dynamics of the mind and insist on the need to understand how personality develops from infancy onwards; all accept the concept of repression and unconscious mental activity. In other words they are based upon Freud's original work. In the practice of psychotherapy all aim to deal with emotional conflict, conscious or unconscious, and the methods of treatment do not vary greatly from one school to another. In saying that pastoral counselling derives from psychoanalysis I am aware that all the schools of psychotherapy have made their contribution, but the differences in the aims and methods of counselling are far less marked than in psychotherapy. In trying to explain the principles governing pastoral counselling I shall use the concepts of the Freudian school, not merely because they are fundamental to the whole development of analytic therapy, but because I have found them the most convincing in explaining human behaviour in general and in the particular field of religion. I make no apology for doing so, for I am convinced that this is the most satisfactory approach, and a consistent theory is necessary to explain how and why counselling and pastoral care can be made effective. Those who are not as convinced as I am of the validity of psychoanalytic theories will, I am sure, find little difficulty in adjusting what I have to say to the psychologies which they have found most helpful and illuminating.

Psychoanalysis began as a method of healing. Freud was seeking a satisfactory method of treating hysteria, and after a thoroughgoing investigation into all the known methods he took up a case in which his teacher, Professor Breuer, had achieved what he called "a talking cure". This led Freud to study more closely the dynamics of the mind and he was able to refine on the method, first by the use of hypnotism and then by free association. Breuer had achieved the first cure but he had not understood the processes which brought it about. Soon Freud developed both the technique of treatment and also the psychological theories which gave meaning to the technique and explained the nature of the illness treated. The combination of technique and theory he called "psychoanalysis". From these first beginnings both the techniques of treatment and the body of theory on which they depend have undergone extensive development, by Freud himself, by his orthodox followers, and by many who have turned aside from the main line of psychoanalysis but who can be regarded as contributors to dynamic psychology.

It is significant that the teaching of psychoanalysis is still predominantly carried out in the medical schools rather than in the departments of psychology in the universities. Freud himself made sundry ventures into the psychoanalytic interpretation of religion, art, sociology, and literature, and his example has been followed by others, but in general such essays have been regarded as *tours de force*, successful or unsuccessful, by-products of an activity whose main aim is elsewhere. The major emphasis has always been on the practical, even where the theories of psychoanalysis have been taken up by educationists. The theory has naturally been regarded as important, but chiefly as justifying the technique in medicine, education, or other fields. This emphasis is reflected in religion. The uprush of interest in pastoral counselling, which we have noted, stems from the desire to make use of techniques modelled on those of psychotherapy, and there is a rapidly growing interest also in the application of psychoanalysis to the aims and methods of religious education. But the reinterpretation of religious beliefs in the light of psychoanalytic knowledge meets little enthusiasm, and a large proportion, if not the majority, of the books on the theory of religion take a defensive attitude of resistance against what is thought of as the "challenge" of psychoanalysis to the understanding of religion and what it stands for.

Because this attitude of defensive resistance in doctrinal matters is so prevalent, most clergy are apt to fall into it consciously or unconsciously. The pastoral counsellor in his specialist role will possibly be trained out of it, but the parish priest will have less thorough training and the circumstances of his work will press him in two opposite directions. In such efforts at counselling that he will be called on to make, he will take advantage of the new insights from psychoanalysis; in his preaching and teaching he will, as an official of his Church—apart from what his own personal convictions may be—be expected to propound and defend the older ideas. This tension between the two aspects of his work can easily create difficulties for the pastor, but it serves a useful purpose if he takes due note of it, for it will help him to understand that his training is not primarily to equip him with a technique that he can apply to those coming to him for counsel, but that the training is first of all aimed to produce the right attitudes in himself by giving him insight into his own emotional difficulties, of which he is probably unaware, and some opportunity to overcome them. He must be able to counsel himself before he can counsel others. Before he can accept others he must accept himself. That is why a personal analysis is necessary in the training of a psychotherapist and almost as necessary in a specialist counsellor.

It was the discovery of the unconscious part of the mind that opened the way for Freud to develop psychoanalysis. In it he found the root causes of the hysterias which he was investigating and, after experimenting, often successfully, with hypnotism as a method of recovering buried memories, he devised the technique of free association characteristic of psychoanalysis. When in particular he applied it to dream interpretation he found, as he says, "the royal road to the unconscious". The unconscious is unconscious because there is an active force keeping it out of the reach of the conscious mind. This force is repression and it should be noted at once and always borne in mind that repression works unconsciously. We can never observe it at work in ourselves and therein it differs from ordinary self-control or suppression of our impulses. Repression also works in the reverse direction; that is, any attempt, by psychoanalysis or otherwise, to unveil the unconscious material is resisted vigorously, by evasion of all kinds, by anger, by fear, by anxiety that threatens to overwhelm the self, even in some cases by suicide. A young woman of my acquaintance under the pressure of probing enquiries passionately declared that she would rather commit suicide than face what she felt to be in her unconscious mind. The strength of the repressing force is shown most clearly when it is met as resistance to exposure of unconscious material in analysis, and in turn that strength shows how powerful are the contents of the unconscious mind since so much energy is required to contain them. The unconscious is not a cellar or lumber room where unwanted things are put out of the way to lie neglected and forgotten and to moulder away. It is much more like a battle-field where two armies are at constant war, but unlike other wars the armies do not destroy or weaken each other. The battle in the mind is never-ending. The forces of the unconscious seek to take possession of the mind and body and so get out into open expression; the repressing force keeps them contained to the utmost of ability. The psychotherapist or counsellor appears in part to be on the side of the repressed forces, so the repressing forces put up equal resistance against him.

Metaphors such as this are bound to be misleading. To speak of a battle is too spatial and too anthropomorphic. Even to speak of a repressing force is inaccurate, for what we have is two parts of the total self (total includes the conscious and the unconscious) struggling against each other in the unconscious mind. For full health and vigour of the personality they should be brought into harmony. This in the end can only be achieved by a proper balance between the conscious mind and the two forces at war in the unconscious. What that proper balance is and how it may be achieved has to be discussed. Some things are clear. One is that the conscious mind has to gain access to much that is otherwise unconscious, that is, that repression and resistance have to be undone, and this means open acknowledgement by the self of much of what it is endeavouring in the battle in the unconscious to reject.

In a later chapter we shall examine more precisely the nature and aims of the battling forces of the mind. At this point I want to follow up the consequences of the fact to which I drew attention just now, that the contending forces in the battle cannot destroy or weaken each other. At the most they can hold each other in check. What almost invariably happens, however, is that they reach a compromise, or series of compromises, by which each side gains what it seeks. The repressed forces take on a disguise and present themselves to the scrutiny of the repressing forces in a new shape. In the new shape they are no longer objectionable and are allowed through to consciousness and to expression, but they are not allowed to resume their native form. They must maintain the guise they have assumed or another which is permitted. There are a number of psychological mechanisms—displacement, identification, alogical association, projection, symbolization, etc.—which make possible an infinite variety of disguises. The compromise between repressing and repressed is an attempt to reach the ideal solution of harmonization between the different parts of the mind or person.

Tension and conflict between different parts of the mind is not bad in itself. It is inevitable and even essential to growth, a sign of life. Periods of severe inner struggle, as in the Oedipus Complex stage of early childhood and in adolescence, are the preliminaries to development of the personality. This comes by resolving the conflict. Without such struggles we cannot attain the highest levels of human personality. At various periods in his life Jesus wrestled with conflicts in his mind. The Agony in the Garden was such an occasion. So were the Temptations. These were not a sign of weakness but of strength, for he could bring the conflict in himself into the open in full awareness. Badness lies in the manner of dealing with the inner conflict. By resorting to repression we are denying the possibility of resolving the tension, of finding a positive or constructive way out. We are trying, in vain of course, to run away from the pain which it brings or from the renunciation which it seems to demand. The consequences are disastrous. The conflict, though hidden in the unconscious, goes on there as violently as ever, exhausting the energies of the mind, arresting the growth—and sometimes even the functioning—of the self, and forcing the compromises to which I have referred. These take the form of neurotic illnesses, incapacitating the sufferer from carrying on a normal life, aberrations of character, exaggerated traits of conduct, irrational fears and anxieties, inability to maintain normal social relations, or the countless other signs of unresolved unconscious conflict.

The counsellor or psychotherapist has to help the sufferer to become aware of and to face the conflicts which he has been hiding from himself. But he is hindered in his effort by the fact that he as well as his "client" (to adopt Carl Rogers' term in place of the misleading "patient" or awkward "counselee") has an unconscious mind. We are all quite ready to give intellectual assent to the assertion that everyone, including ourselves, has an active unconscious mind. Intellectual assent, however, does not solve the dynamic problems created by our unconscious and may even serve to protect the unconscious still further from recognition, by misleading us into supposing that such intellectual acceptance *is* recognition of it. If the counsellor has not come to terms with his own repressions they will not only create blind spots or distortions in his understanding of his client's needs, they may even become active barriers repelling the client so that the latter's own repressions are as it were strengthened by those of the counsellor. Hence before anyone can become a good counsellor, or pastor, he must be able to deal with his own unconscious conflicts; that is, he must become conscious of them and find ways to solve them. This is why he undergoes training. It will be emphasized over and over again in the following pages that the basic aim of training is not to acquire a method of handling cases but to enable the would-be pastor to discover his own motives and solve his own conflicts. The method he uses will flow out of this. Pastoral care and counselling must not be thought of in impersonal terms of casework, but as a personal relationship creating a situation of a special kind, in which the client is enabled to win freedom from the paralysing effects of his unconscious motives by the help and understanding the pastor gives to him. Both must live through the difficulties the client is suffering from, so the pastor must have solved his own emotional problems if he is to lead his client to the way of healthy growth. His training therefore is shaped to enable him to discover himself in personal relations.

The recognition of this principle is shown in the development of the practice of psychoanalysis. Freud first described it as the science of the unconscious and concentrated on finding the best technique for penetrating into the unconscious of his patients, evolving free association and the analysis of dreams. As psychoanalysis developed more emphasis came to be laid on the transference which develops in the patient, that is, the focusing on the analyst, by projection, of unconscious emotional attitudes held by the patient towards his parents, formed by him in infancy, and repressed. The transference enables the patient to live through his infantile feelings again and to outgrow them as, through analysis, the meaning of the transference is made clear. But transference is not only positive. It has a strong negative aspect. The analyst is trying to open up the material which has been repressed, so there is a strong resistance set up in the patient, corresponding to the force of the repression. The resistance manifests itself in many ways, including opposition to the analyst. The next stage, therefore, was to emphasize the need of dealing with the resistance. After that the importance of the counter-transference was recognized. The analyst has his own problems, his own unconscious motives, and these come to be active in his relations to his patient. Hence it was seen that the analyst needs to analyse himself as well as his patient in the course of the analysis. He cannot be entirely objective. He is also subjective in the analytical situation. Analysis is a relationship between two persons. The analyst has to lead but both are involved in a living situation in which two people confront each other and by sharing commit themselves to each other. It is the building up of this mutual self-committal and sharing which in the end gives the strength needed by the patient and enables him to find healing. The personal problems encountered by the pastor, at least those with which he can deal and to which he should confine his efforts, are not so deep-seated as those requiring full analysis, but the healing factor is the same, the trustful relationship reached between client and pastor.

The methods to be adopted in counselling are subordinate to this relationship and flow out of it. They will be spelled out in more detail as we proceed and the justification for them is made plainer. At this point only a general description is necessary. They should be non-directive and client-centred.[1] The counsellor does not set out to advise and direct his client, but to listen to him and to encourage him to talk freely. He knows that his client is troubled by unconscious conflicts and that therefore the story as told to him is far from the complete one and may be heavily distorted. He does not blame the client for this, nor intervene to correct

[1] See Carl Rogers, *Counselling and Psychotherapy*, and *Client-Centered Therapy*.

him. The blindness and the distortion are part of his trouble. Correcting him, or rebuking him, however mildly, only serves to drive the client back into himself and makes it harder for him to see where his real trouble lies. The counsellor must aim to enable the client to get at the motives in him which were previously unconscious or unrecognized and of which he has been afraid. Some of the fear is taken away by the welcoming non-judgmental attitude of the counsellor, for the client has been judging himself harshly and expects the counsellor to pass the same judgment on him. When the latter accepts him as he is and treats him as someone worth giving time to, his own self-criticism is eased and he can talk more freely and it will become possible for him to bring into the open feelings and thoughts which hitherto he has been afraid to acknowledge. This is further facilitated when the counsellor, instead of making comments on what the client says to him, shows that he understands what the client has been saying and feeling by repeating, perhaps in other words or by selecting significant phrases from what has been said, what the client has been meaning and particularly feeling. This clarification usually enables the client to move forward another step.

In this way the counsellor reflects like a mirror the state of mind of the client and enables him to see himself, and his problems, more clearly. To do this the counsellor needs to be able to enter into his client's mind, to think and feel like him and to accept what he finds. His chief effort will be directed to this. Since he is, we must assume (but see Chapter 7), free from the bondage to which the client is subject in his unconscious, he lives out a healthy attitude to the problems which the client has found insoluble and the latter is enabled to find his true self in the counsellor's view of him and grow into it. The counsellor's function and his technique is to love and to listen to his client. In that way the true personal relationship develops and expands. The client, the one in need, is provided with the setting he needs to come to a knowledge of himself and to find healing.

3

Healing and the Pastoral Encounter

In his work as a counsellor the pastor is frequently tempted, especially before he has gained adequate experience, to try to do more than he appears to be doing. Results are not coming quickly enough. He thinks he understands the nature of the problem and can see what the solution is, but somehow he cannot get it across to the client. He feels an urge to intervene in his client's talk, to explain things to him, to give him advice either moral or psychological, to press him to understand the causes of his trouble. He may do this because of his own temperament or character, in which case he is unfitted to be a counsellor, though that which unfits him may also make him the more eager to be one. I shall say something about this in Chapter 7. He may fall into error, however, because, as we have just seen, he has mistaken the nature of counselling. He has been badly trained and tries to use counselling as a method of manipulating the psychological and spiritual life of his client. There is another reason why he fails as a counsellor, namely, that he has not made sufficient allowance for the innate urge in his client to growth and health, and feels that it is his responsibility to push his client on.

The concept of *vis medicatrix naturae*, the healing force of nature, is accepted without question with respect to our bodies. The body builds new tissues to heal wounds, repairs broken bones, creates anti-bodies to fight off bacteria and viruses, and so on. Often what appears as the symptom of some disease is at the same time the sign of the body's struggle to restore health. High temperature results from the effort to counter infection, or pus from the marshalling of the body's resources to throw out invaders or foreign matter. The physician and surgeon simply try to provide the best conditions for the innate powers of the body to do their healing work.

The same healing force operates in the realm of the mind. Its work is not perceptible by the sense organs and it can therefore be forgotten or overlooked. Freud drew attention to it in formulating his theory of life and death "instincts", perhaps the most obscure and certainly the most confusing of his theories.[1] We need not take up his theory here, but it ought to be mentioned because it is central to religious concerns of life and death (cf. Deut. 30). As with the symptoms of bodily disease the symptoms of mental disorder reveal an inner struggle to achieve control as well as giving a clue to the nature of the disorder. Hysterical symptoms are a compromise between the repressing forces and the repressed material, just as fever is the result of the body's struggles to overcome an infection. Freud very early in his work suggested that schizophrenia should be seen as the struggle of the mind to regain normal health rather than as an illness in itself. Doctors frequently encounter this inner force in the form of "the will to live", which on occasion seems to enable a patient to recover from a degree of illness or injury which in most cases would prove fatal.

I have referred to this innate factor as a force. That is undoubtedly a misconception. It is an aspect of the whole life process, not one of the subordinate elements within it, such as sight or the instinct of anger. It enters into every manifestation of life, bodily and mental. If it is not there we are dead, just as parts of our body cease to be restored and die. Whether there is a corresponding death process is a more difficult question, but it is a misnomer to call either

---

[1] *Beyond the Pleasure Principle* (Hogarth Press).

life or death an instinct. An instinct is one among a group of innate functions of the whole person, driving towards activities which follow patterns, of varied preciseness, inherited by the individual. The drive of the instincts is part of the life process and life is not an additional drive. It is a mode of organization of matter (and mind) characterizing the living organism as self-maintaining, self-repairing, self-reproducing. Death may be a separate characteristic, but it is enough for our purposes to see it as the cessation, for whatever reason, of these life activities. By speaking of a life force we are merely emphasizing the special characteristics which distinguish living from non-living things. If we keep them in mind it will be simpler and less misleading to speak of life or life force instead of life instinct.

For the purposes of pastoral care we need to take account of two aspects of life—healing and growth. I said that the healing drive works in the mind as well as in the body. This distinction between mind and body is drawn only for convenience of discussion; it is not absolute. The nature of the link between body and mind is a mystery that has not been solved and probably cannot be solved without considerable change in our scientific and philosophical assumptions. Existence, life, as we know it, is psychosomatic. It seems clear that the mind depends on the body and it is probably as equally true that the body—as a living body—depends upon the mind. What happens to or in the body affects the mind, and all the activities of the mind are associated with changes in the body. Mental disorders, whether severe or mild, have their bodily concomitants, and there is a school of thought which inclines to the theory that all mental disorder is due to a malfunctioning of the body on the chemical, glandular, or some other physiological level. This theory is very far from being established and on the other side there is a great body of evidence to indicate that many cases of mental disorder, and even many in which the symptoms are of a physical character, are caused by mental, or psychological, factors. Only further research and experience will determine what is the truth, but in the meanwhile we are justified in acting on the assumption that in some types of case the causes of the trouble are of a psychological character and that psychological remedies are needed to heal them. This is the justification for psychotherapy and pastoral care and counselling. The selection of the right psychological treatment demands as much skill as does the practice of bodily medicine.

Pastoral care, whatever the motivating urge to it may be and whatever the ultimate aim of the pastor, must be seen as part of the total complex of psychological healing and subject to the same conditions for its success. This means that the pastor must give paramount importance to the innate urge to health in his client. His client's personality must be his primary consideration. Someone comes to him seeking help. Only by a change in the balance of forces active in his personality can the difficulties of the client be overcome, so the pastor's aim must be to help him achieve the change. But the pastor cannot remake the client. He can only help him to overcome his own mental difficulties by providing the right conditions for the innate urge to health to work more effectively. He may carry in his mind the pattern of an ideal man, drawn from many sources, theological or otherwise, and will be tempted to try to impose this ideal upon his client. The attempt to do so is bound to fail for the double reason that the pattern is certain to be in conflict with the already established pattern in the client's personality and that the method used to impose it will frustrate his inner struggle to grow into health. By such methods, even where there is some apparent amelioration in the client's situation, the latter is likely to be brought into an even worse condition than before he sought help. Pastoral care, therefore, must aim at liberating people from their own difficulties, enabling them to be their true selves, to realize the full potentialities of their natural endowment. They can only be helped to solve their own problems and this will not be by any attempt to get them to conform to pre-determined patterns of conduct.

This brings us to the second aspect of life which sound pastoral care must consider, namely, that of growth. The difficulties which bring people to seek help are always matters of defective growth. Either they are unable to resolve current conflicts, current demands upon their mental resources, or they have undergone some aberration of growth in the past which weakens them in frequently recurring situations. When some situation occurs in which they appear to be called upon to make decisions, to accept a load of responsibility, to face likely renunciation or pain or insecurity, they react to it, not in the light of the current demands, but as if it were the earlier one in which the weakness was first established. Almost invariably the first situation belonged to early childhood and had to do with emotional relations with the parents. Failure to solve the early crisis leaves them with a fixation in an infantile attitude and they tend to approach every serious problem with this attitude. They cannot solve current difficulties unless they are set free from the infantile fixation.

Psychotherapy and pastoral care aim at helping them to win through to freedom. Some methods of psychotherapy aim directly at uncovering the early fixation. This requires highly trained skill and is not a method which pastors should try to follow. On the other hand sympathetic counselling in a current difficulty usually helps the client to get insight into the character of his behaviour so that he comes to understand that he is behaving in an infantile way, trying to recreate an infantile situation, and seeking infantile solutions. Insight then helps him to win to a greater degree of inner freedom and to grow to greater maturity of outlook. The pastor needs to be alert to the fact that his client is not only behaving in an infantile way—this is usually fairly clear—but also is unconscious that he is doing so. His need is for help to solve the earlier problem but in the context of the one he is at present facing. To tell him that he is behaving as an infant is useless and may even be harmful. He needs help to grow. Hence the pastor should understand the stages of normal growth and have some knowledge of how and when that growth is most likely to be interrupted.

I have discussed this in more detail elsewhere with special reference to religion,[1] and will only give the main points here. The reference to religion is important in its bearing upon pastoral work and I shall have more to say about it in Chapter 10. At this point we should concentrate on pastoral care as promoting the inward development of the client, without any discussion of its religious implications.

It is convenient to divide the life of a man (or woman) into six stages: infancy (0–5), childhood (6–12), adolescence (13–19), adulthood (20–45), maturity (45–65), senescence (65–   ). The length of these stages varies according to the individual and the years indicated should not be taken as exact for any given person. The first three periods are more precise than the others. They are the ones which affect development most, but there are pastoral problems associated with the second three. Indeed the parish priest is likely to find that most of the problems brought to him will appear to belong to these stages, even if on examination he finds that inadequate development in the early stages has predisposed the client to failure in later life. Obviously the duration given for these last three periods should allow for considerable variation. Between the early stages there is a period of fairly rapid transition, but usually there is partial overlap from one stage to another. The stages follow each other as the unfolding of an inner constitutional drive to growth. The inner urge, however, does not and cannot operate in a vacuum, for no one can grow up in isolation from the world and other people, so the growth is conditioned by the circumstances of the individual's upbringing, especially in the first five years, and these may hinder or promote the growth.

[1] See *Your Growing Child and Religion* (Penguin Books 1965), and *Freud and Christianity* (Penguin Books 1967).

Hindrance means some degree of arrested growth and the norm of mental health is unhindered growth.

The result of a healthy development is to produce the complex structure of human personality at its highest level of functioning. The different stages, certainly the first four, each contribute something characteristic of the stage to the final result. In this sense, therefore, the human personality is not fully formed until adulthood. Arrest in one of the early stages means that some essential element is lacking from the final result. We run up against the ambiguities of language here. Every person is of course a member of the species *homo* and is entitled to be called a man, but if he has failed to actualize the potentialities with which he is endowed he has in another sense fallen short of manhood. It is with this second meaning that we are concerned here. We may be tempted to lay down *a priori* criteria for what manhood comprises, criteria which are based on social, ethical, or theological assumptions. They imply that a man ought to conform to the generally accepted conventions or standards of social intercourse, show courtesy, good manners, consideration for other people; that he ought to try to live a good life, following what is believed right and refusing to do wrong; or that he should be obedient to God and pursue the life of the spirit. It is assumed that because he ought to do these things he can do them. "Thou oughtest, therefore thou canst." The temptation therefore is to point out what ought to be done and to rely on encouragement, persuasion, and exhortation to bring the client to do it.

This is to mistake the nature of a man's freedom to act. It presupposes that a man is a unified personality with all his motivations accessible to control by his will power and that his failures in conduct are due to ignorance, which may be corrected by instruction, or to weakness of will, which can be fortified by encouragement, exhortation, and, if need be, by the threat of punishment. We fall into this error because this is how we commonly perceive ourselves. We may in fact be adequately integrated persons, having no major mental conflicts to trouble us and assume that other people are like ourselves. But it may well be that we have our aberrations of behaviour and are unaware of them or construe them wrongly becaused they are rooted in our unconscious. We do not perceive the real motives of our behaviour since they are cut off from consciousness. Instead we invent reasons to explain it or over-emphasize secondary motives. This is the well-known process of "rationalization". This gives a false sense of control and of unity and hides the division in ourselves.

Unity of personality is not something given to us from the beginning. We begin with the raw materials of personality and growing into a mature, unified mind is a long and sometimes painful process which continues throughout life as experience brings ever new material to be assimilated. The great contribution of modern psychology has been to uncover the stages of this development, to reveal the ways in which it goes wrong, and to suggest ever improving ways of avoiding or correcting the failures. This opens the way for an empirical approach to pastoral care based on the positive scientific study of what actually happens in the growth of persons from birth onwards and of the dynamics of interpersonal relations. The new approach replaces the older paternalistic and authoritative way.

In the next few chapters we shall examine some of the particular weaknesses and failures of development which most frequently occur in the early stages of growth and the part the pastor can play in trying to remedy them, but before we come to the detail there are some general features of the pastoral relationship of which the successful pastor must be constantly aware if he is to avoid succumbing to the dangers to which they will constantly expose him. They depend partly on the client, partly on the pastor, and they become active as soon as someone comes to the pastor for help and the pastor tries to give it.

Consider the client. He needs help because he is in some kind of difficulty. It may be that he is incapacitated by fears, anxieties, or depressions, or he may be unable to manage his personal relations with other people, his wife, parents, or children. He may find it a strain to meet new people or be tormented by his feeling of inadequacy at social gatherings. He may be plagued by feelings of guilt and worthlessness, sometimes for reasons which will seem to the pastor insufficient to explain the depth of the feelings. Whatever his trouble is it points to mal-development. He has not grown up fully. He is part child, part adult. Infantile attitudes and aims persist in him and he cannot let them go. Because they are irreconcilable with adult attitudes they have to be repressed so that he is unaware of them and cannot recognize what is governing part of his behaviour. Behaviour that is natural and proper in a young child is out of place in an adult. It contravenes the law of life and growth. This does not deny the value of child-likeness in an adult, manifested in directness, trust, faith, interest in other people, which mark the behaviour of the child, for these attitudes are on a different level in the adult. It is the persistence of the attitudes unchanged, that is, childishness, which is the trouble. He is, as it were, two persons trying to be one but unable to achieve it. Yet he does not know what is the real cause of his trouble and will not easily be brought to face it.

When, therefore, he comes for help he brings both persons, the infant and the adult in him. It is, of course, not accurate to regard him as two persons, except in the very rare cases of multiple personality. Rather, it is a matter of incompatible aspects of an incompletely integrated personality. Nevertheless it is sometimes useful to think of two personalities either of which may dominate the behaviour of the client at any given time or in particular contexts, giving reasonably adult or infantile attitudes as the case may be. Both will be active at all times, but the infantile aspect, being repressed and unconscious, may be hidden and mask itself in adult forms, protected, as we have seen, by rationalizations. When he comes to the pastor the adult in him will present the case in terms of the problem which has precipitated his need, but his emotional attitudes to the pastor will be dominated by the infantile aspect of the personality. He will tend to treat the pastor as a parent surrogate and adopt towards him the attitudes of a young child to his parents, dependence and love, fear and rebelliousness. He will unconsciously seek from the pastor the satisfactions he failed to get from his parents, the assurance of unbroken love, understanding and forgiveness of his failures and his weakness, protection against his fears, security against everything that seems to threaten him, particularly the prospect of suffering mental pain, of having to make decisions and assume responsibilities, or of undergoing frustration and deprivation. He will exaggerate the wisdom and the goodness of the pastor and will try to induce him to make all the decisions and run his life for him. At the same time as he treats the pastor as the ideal parent, he is liable to see him as in infancy he saw his actual parents and the emotions they raised in him will be revived and transferred on to the pastor, emotions of anger and hostility, of fear and rebelliousness, of jealousy and guilt and, above all, the desire to get the mastery of them, the parents, by any means possible.

This revival of infantile attitudes and emotions in relation to the pastor is called the transference, or transference situation. Psychoanalysts are familiar with it and make use of it as one of the means of therapy since analysis of it enables them to bring infantile conflicts to light. This requires highly developed skills beyond the capacity of the ordinary pastor, who must deal with the transference in ways adapted to his training and his function. The clients who come to him will be the less incapacitated and therefore less fixed in infantile attitudes than those who need treatment by a psychotherapist. That is, the transference in them, while it is certain to occur, will not be so violent as it is with those needing psychotherapy. The pastor should be able to bring his client to consciousness of his infantile motives without recourse to analysis. To succeed, however, he must be aware of and deal with the counter-transference, that is, the transference on to the client of the pastor's own unconscious infantile attitudes, and his reactions to the infantile behaviour of the client towards him.

The fact that he is the pastor, that he is professionally accredited to his office and is supposed to be competent to help his parishioners, does not automatically do away with the power of his own unconscious motives. Nor does his intellectual assent to the idea that he has unconscious motives make him directly aware of them. If he is to be good at pastoral care it is important that he accept the certainty that he, like his client, has repressions which shape his behaviour. No one is entirely free from them. As we shall see in Chapter 7 he is likely to have chosen his vocation partly under the influence of such unconscious motives. He will therefore be well-advised to watch his reactions to his client. For instance, he must not become irritated by his client's continued practice of saying one thing and doing another, or by his evasiveness, or by the client's unpunctuality. He must not be disappointed but alerted by apparent failure to elicit appropriate response and progress on the part of the client. On the other hand he should not be misled into taking the client's praises seriously. The client will almost invariably adopt an attitude of dependence, seeking advice about decisions he has to make, or about social relationships or work, apparently placing himself with the utmost trust in the hands of the pastor. The latter should beware lest his own unconscious needs lead him to accept the role thus offered to him. On the one hand if he does so he will only confirm the client in his infantile attitudes, and on the other he is likely to find his advice flouted, since by accepting the role he has put himself in the power of the client and allowed himself to be manipulated, and the client will now call the tune. Further, the adult part of the client has sought help to escape from the infantile part, and to give way to the latter is to refuse the former. These are only a few examples of how the pastor may be misled by his own unconscious needs. Perhaps the commonest trap into which he may fall is that mentioned at the beginning of the chapter, namely, the assumption, and also the desire, that he should actively direct the course of the interviews with the client, that it is up to him to tell the client how to overcome his difficulties.

The role of the pastor is to stimulate and assist the working of the inner forces of healing in the client. The latter is unable to bear the stresses which the circumstances of his life are putting upon him because of his inner weaknesses caused through his failure to grow through some phases of his infancy and attain full integration and maturity of personality. He needs to be assisted to grow again. The pastor must recognize the dual aspect of his client. He accepts the fact of the infantilisms and does not criticize his client for them. But he does not approve of them as a satisfactory state of being for the client. He sympathizes with him in his efforts to get free of them and the difficulties they create. He addresses himself to the adult part of the client, leaving it to him to make decisions, and aims to assist him in this, first by helping him to understand his own motives and second by not criticizing or condemning him when he makes what to the pastor seem to be bad decisions. By listening with sympathy and respect for the client's right to independence he usually enables him to get deeper and deeper understanding of his true motives, and with that understanding the power to grow again and face the pressures from within and without.

This is not an easy task to undertake. What is involved in it will become clearer as we examine in the next chapters some of the failures in growth and the reasons why they occur.

4

Problems from Early Infancy

The period of infancy is the most important because in it the basic attitudes and the general structure of the personality are formed. Any deviations from the general overall pattern to be found in a given individual have their roots in infancy. The infant's mind at birth is not formed; he has only the capacity to think and feel and his mind only functions in response to stimuli which will come to him from within or without his body. In other words, just as his body grew in his mother's womb from a tiny cell, so his mind has to grow from a minute beginning until it has all the richness and complexity of the mind of a mature man. The setting of the family in the first few years corresponds to the womb, and the resolution of the Oedipus Complex, which takes place, roughly, over the period five to seven years of age, is analogous to the process of birth. The food on which the mind grows consists of the experiences he undergoes. The pattern the mind takes depends on the nature of these experiences as they are worked over by the constitutional urge to absorb and unify them. Human beings have a long period of growing up mentally as well as bodily. The rich mental development is possible only because the mind is not set at birth into fixed forms but is plastic, with only the main lines of growth pre-patterned, so that within the broad pre-determined pattern an infinite variety of lesser patterns can be found. Learning by experience means receiving and storing knowledge; it also means acquiring a shape to the mind.

The plasticity which is the condition of learning at the

same time renders possible mal-development in growth. Another factor facilitating mal-development is that it takes many years for the individual to acquire an adequate grasp of language. Language is the greatest tool man has developed, for communication, for formulation of experiences, for storing knowledge. It is a means of interior unification of experiences. In counselling, half the work or more is done when the client is able to verbalize and communicate his feelings. But many of his most significant experiences take place before he has learned language and with it the power to objectify what he is undergoing. Hence conflicts, dissociations, repressions, occur most easily in infancy. The profounder aspects of these is the realm of the psychotherapist. The pastor needs only to be aware of the more general features.

The period of infancy comprises three sub-stages—the mother-child phase, the rise of the Oedipus Complex, and the resolution of the Oedipus Complex. The first of these begins at birth (possibly even in the womb) and continues until about the age of two years, when normally the young child comes to self-consciousness, that is, awareness of himself as a person over against another person, his mother. It is difficult, if not impossible, for an adult to think back and perceive by introspection the character of consciousness in this pre-personal period in which there cannot be an awareness of self as the experiencing subject over against objects perceived as the ground or cause of the experiences. Certain states of mind, however, such as some forms of mystical experience, depersonalized or trans-personalized consciousness under the influence of psychedelic drugs, and states of mind sometimes occurring in mental disorders, are at least analogous to pre-personal consciousness and may be the result of regression to this form of mental activity. But even if this latter supposition is correct, the regression is to the early form of thinking and later experiences are translated into it so that what emerges is not entirely the revival of experiences undergone in the first period of life. We cannot be sure that these occasional states give us reliable information about pre-personal thinking, but the intensity of the experiences they bring with them may be a valuable clue. The infant is unaware of his separate identity but nevertheless he is a separate centre of consciousness. His mind therefore is the *mélange* of sensations, perceptions, feelings, he is living through and which he gradually reduces to order. Frequently recurring experiences must gradually become recognized and built into chains or groups, whereas others which occur less frequently and with less intensity of feeling will remain in the confused penumbra surrounding the central pattern. The experiences associated with his mother and those with his body will be the groups first sorted out from the confusion and these will gradually be developed into the recognition of himself over against his mother. At some point this bursts into full self-consciousness, the sense of being a separate person.

The importance of this period for the development of the individual and the need for pastoral counsellors to understand what may go wrong in it has been recently emphasized by Dr Frank Lake, on the one hand, in his massive work on *Clinical Theology,* and, on the other, by Professor John Macmurray, in his Gifford Lectures, *Persons in Relation.* It is in this period that the schizoid personality originates with its characteristic splitting. Whether the splitting (from which the adjective "schizoid" is derived) is the division of an ego which was in the first instance unitary, or whether it represents the failure to bind experience together into an integrated unitary ego-self, is a question too profound for us to attempt an answer here. But the pastor who does not wish to attempt psychotherapy but only to give proper care to his clients will understand his own role if he grasps the basic features of this pre-personal stage. Some will seek his help with difficulties which originate in the failure to get through the stage successfully and achieve a strong ego, and for them he will have to be a mother substitute with whom they can re-live it more successfully. Three points in particular are important to guide him.

The first of these is the social aspect of the development. The individual does not begin in separation and then enter into social relations with other people. This is how as adults we feel ourselves behaving, aware of our separateness and of having to reach out or respond to other persons. But we begin life in a social matrix in which we cannot yet distinguish self and other; in which indeed self is not yet formed. It is out of this social matrix of mother and baby that the self-identity of the baby is gradually formed. We are social beings before we are individuals. Our individuality depends upon this social context. If we have a weakened or defective personality which hampers us in social relationships, excessive timidity or assertiveness, for instance, it is almost certainly because we have not passed successfully through the pre-personal stage and so have failed to achieve an integrated self.

It is easy for something to go wrong. The mother-baby relationship is not symmetrical. The mother is a developed person, aware of her own identity, taking separateness for granted. She has a multitude of interests of which the baby is only one. The baby's mind is unformed, still embryonic so far as personality is concerned, and he is only aware of his experiences without any perception of a world standing over against himself. To grow into a person he needs to be treated as a person, helped to develop into what his innate endowments predispose him to become. It is easy for the mother and others in the family to treat him as a thing rather than as a person because of his immaturity and helplessness, and because of the pressure of other demands upon her time and attention. When that happens he is not called on to respond as a person and his inner need is not met. Further, if the mother herself has in some way fallen short of developing a fully integrated personality, if, for instance, she feels insecure in social relationships, she is bound to betray this in her treatment of the baby. She may vacillate between love and neglect, be over-demanding of response, be impatient and scolding, and all this will leave its impress on the emerging personality of the baby, either directly or by reaction. We are shaped by the society in which we grow, as is shown by the children who, reared by wolves, became wolves. The urge to grow is constitutionally innate; it cannot be forced from without, but the social environment conditions it and can induce defects of structure and function in the resulting personality. The sins of the fathers (and mothers) are visited upon the children unto the third and fourth generations. This is a natural, not a moral or theological, law.

It should be clear, then, why effective pastoral care is basically a personal relationship, a meeting of persons. Certainly the pastor must treat his client throughout as a person, never as a "case". Of course statistically he is a case, but to treat him primarily as an object on which to employ techniques of treatment is to de-personalize him and defeat from the beginning the aim of the treatment. This is true even where the technique learned is to treat the client as a person. In other words, the pastor must enter into a genuine and not an assumed personal encounter with his client. Everything else is subsidiary to this. But again, as with mother and baby, it is an unbalanced relationship. We must assume that the pastor has attained a greater degree of maturity, of mental and spiritual health, than his client, for it is his mal-development that brings the latter to him. Whether this assumption is always valid will be discussed at a later point (see Chapter 7). The pastor is supplying what the client missed in his pre-personal stage and providing the stimulus and the setting for the correction of the defect of development. A psychotherapist dealing with severe cases would probably have to take his patient back over the early period, but the pastor will find that he can do much to set his client free in helping him to deal with current difficulties. If he cannot, he should pass him on to a psychotherapist. In every case the encounter between pastor and client is on at least two levels. The grown-up man (or woman) seeks the help of the pastor over immediate problems, such as his difficulty in making satisfying contact with other people. But underneath this lies the infantile personality weakened by failure to develop an integrated identity and unconsciously treating the pastor as a mother and behaving towards him in the dependent fashion of a baby towards his mother. Two attitudes will conflict, sometimes alternate, in him. On the one hand, because his ego has been left weak in infancy he will be afraid to face the demands the world makes upon him and he will seek protection. Openly or mutely he will expect the pastor to make the decisions for him, bear the responsibility for his actions, advise and guide him and allow him to keep his dependent status, living on the strength, wisdom, and authority of the pastor. On the other hand, the law of growth, the life process, will operate in him, driving him towards achieving a stronger ego, a greater maturity, independence in place of dependence. There is always a danger that the pastor may succumb to the temptation to encourage the dependent attitude, mistaking it as the respect due to his greater learning, wisdom, or experience. By his office he is an authority figure and in his own mind, as well as in the mind of the client, the authority inherent in his office may be transferred to his person. If this happens he cannot do much to help his client. We shall take this up again at a later point when we are considering the motives leading to the choice of a career as a pastor. Here we need only repeat that the aim of the pastor must be to foster the client's growth towards independence.

This means that in most cases, if not all, he will not deliberately try to probe into the repressed infantile unconscious of the client but will confine himself to the current problems the client brings to him. If his sympathetic and understanding attitude leads the client to bring up the earlier material he will, of course, follow him with the same readiness to listen but he will treat the earlier material as part of the current problems rather than the other way round. To stress the causative importance of the infantile experiences is to open the way for the client to take shelter behind them and so to evade accepting the responsibility of making decisions in the present and acting upon them.

Let us pass on to the second feature of this pre-personal stage of development. It is the infant's experience of love, so it is closely inter-woven with the first, the encounter between persons which constitutes the mother-baby relationship.

From birth onwards man needs to love and be loved. The love instincts, whose energy Freud termed the "libido", provide the drive in all his creative activities. These instincts take on a wide range of forms, partly genetically determined, partly resulting from experience. The infinite variety of expression ranges from simple sensual pleasures to the vast pursuits of culture and religion. Libido is the stuff out of which life is made, so it was in the libido that Freud placed what he called the life instinct. Love, as we know it, needs both an object and a response. The infant who has not yet reached awareness of selfhood, and with it awareness of his mother over against him, can only experience love in the pleasures he experiences, the pleasures of taking food, of being held in his mother's arms, of hearing her voice, smelling her breast, and so on, and the pleasures which come from the sensations of his own body. These at first are all vivid sensual pleasures. They are sexual, but in the form of infantile sexuality, which is pre-genital. In this sense the infant is sexually in love with his mother. She on the other hand, has developed the adult form of sexuality, which is one great branch of the all-pervading love-instincts, and which has limited aims and objects of satisfaction, and her love for her baby falls outside this adult sexuality, though it may have sensual pleasures in it, and shows itself as tender emotion and an over-mastering concern for the welfare of the baby. In her response to his need of her she treats him as a person and in so doing she is helping him to develop personality in himself.

The experiences of the infant are not all pleasure-giving.

Some are painful, disturbing, frightening. Hunger, cold, various hurts, illness, loneliness, frustration, and deprivation all can cause him suffering. They appear to attack him, they are something to be avoided. They become grouped together into a constellation of experiences just as the good experiences do. As the pattern of the mother gradually takes shape in his mind she appears alternately as good mother and bad mother. If these are not reconciled in the infant's mind two consequences result. First, the dominance of love and all that that implies in personal attitudes and social relationships is made uncertain. Secondly, the split in the mother will be transferred at a later point to the world and to God. God will appear at times hostile, not always loving, and the world will seem such an unfriendly place and life in it so full of difficulties and suffering that retreat from it may become preferred as the safest mode of behaviour.

The third point to be noted in this pre-personal mother-baby period offers the way of bringing the bad and good mothers into a unity or at any rate of beginning the unification. This lies in the way the mother helps the baby to endure suffering. Some measure of suffering is inevitable and learning to endure it is an essential part of personal growth. It is important, because of the weakness of the infant's growing self, that he should not be asked to bear needless suffering and deprivation, that is, not be left too long cold or hungry or dirty, but be assured by prompt loving attention that love and the pleasures it brings are not destroyed but are certain to come to put an end to the badness. So the infant learns little by little to bear the suffering without panic and even finds that enduring some deprivation increases the pleasures that put an end to it. As he grows he becomes able to accept longer periods and increased intensity of suffering, and pleasure and pain, the goodness and badness of experience, begin to grow together into a whole in which the goodness becomes the dominant partner, and neither the world nor the self, nor God, needs to be split into two.

This integration rarely takes place completely. We all tend to have inner uncertainties about the constancy of love and to fear pain and deprivation. Certainly those who seek help and counsel from the pastor will be suffering in this way. They are likely to be in some measure aware of it, but more likely to have very strong fears buried in their unconscious minds, fears which they are unable to face because they are so personal to themselves. We may rail at the pain in the world and declare it senseless; we may be appalled by the hatreds, the lack of love, prevalent everywhere and condemn the haters; but what dominates us most is our hidden fear that we are unlovable as well as unloved. To be told of a loving God over the world may give some intellectual satisfaction but it does not penetrate to the depths where the real trouble lies in our buried fears and scars of infancy.

The greatest fear of all is the fear of death. This comes when the loss of identity, the uncertainty of personal existence, combines with the loss of love and the fear of suffering. Emptiness, desolation, futility of life, deadness, non-being seem to smother every nascent spark of life, every impulse to joy and to life. We then lack "the courage to be". We may long for extinction to end the emptiness and the despair of living, yet we cannot face extinction, for the life force still tries to drive us forward. We cling instead to false symbols of life and significance, to material prosperity, to renown, social position, even to illness when it makes other people attend to us and gives us the sense of being recognized by them. So we gain some assurance to ourselves that we really exist.

These are the deep needs which pastoral care has to meet. Its aim must be to re-start the growth which has been halted in early infancy or to correct so far as may be possible the distortions of growth which then occurred. It can never be easy. There is no magic formula of explanation or of reasoning to open the closed door; no uplifting exhortation to renew the spirit of life and give courage; no ritual of prayer that will be a substitute for what has to be done. These may accompany or follow but cannot replace the essential steps. The client has to live through his broken infancy again and learn in doing so to grow into wholeness, to find himself, to accept love, and to face suffering instead of running away from it. And to do this he has first to face his own fear about himself, that he is unlovable, that he has no right to exist, no right to accept the interest, love, and friendship which other people offer him.

The pastor's function is to supply what was originally missing, unremitting love, acceptance of him as he is, and interest in him as a person. It needs to be emphasized again that as pastor he ought not to probe into the causes of the client's *malaise*. That is a task for highly skilled psychiatrists and very difficult even for them. If he attempts it the pastor is likely to intensify the secret fears and increase the resistances to getting well. He should rather rely on the inner forces of growth and healing, the urge to life which has brought the client to him, and see himself as the other pole of the relationship which repeats as it were the original mother-baby period in which something went wrong. It cannot be a simple repetition for it will be complicated by all that has happened to the client since his babyhood and by the status and particular character of the pastor. There will be all manner of subsidiary difficulties the client will be wrestling with or afraid of, but basically he will be an infant seeking love, acceptance, and trust by which to become a real person in the world. These the pastor can supply. He must give love, that is, an unselfish concern for the client to become himself, and faith that he can do so. He cannot take over the responsibility of solving the client's problems but he can only help him to do so for himself. The love must be unremitting, that is, it carries acceptance of the client as he is. There must be no condemnation of the client, no hint that he will be loved when he is "good" and not loved when he is "bad", for this perpetuates the division in him which is the very heart of his trouble. He already fears the bad he sees in himself and is overloaded with guilt about it, and needs help to see that it is not really bad but a natural part of himself seen in a false light. If the pastor can see it and still love him he is gradually strengthened to see himself as he really is and to accept what before he was vainly trying to repudiate. The self-mutilation he was inflicting on himself will cease and he will begin to grow again into a more integrated person.

It must not be thought that this is an easy process. First of all the deep fears of the client will drive him to resist, strenuously but unconsciously, the effort to lead him to face the source of his troubles. These fears with the doubts, hesitations, and indecisions that spring from them, will be transferred to more superficial current problems. It is about the latter that he will speak. They will of course be real problems but the pastor should not be surprised if the client is unable to solve them even when to the pastor the solution appears relatively simple. Unconsciously the client sees the basic infantile problem in them. The pastor, being unqualified to deal directly with the underlying causes, must deal with the client in terms of the problem which the latter presents to him. In due course, as trust is built up between them, the client may go on to reveal the deeper troubles and become aware in so doing of the connection between them and the more superficial ones, but the pastor should wait for this to happen of its own accord. It can only take place when the client has built up sufficient strength out of the pastoral relationship to face what he has hitherto been repressing. This requires time and patience on the side of the counsellor.

A second source of difficulty lies in the pastor himself. That he requires patience, and it must be unlimited, we have just noted. We have also seen that he must supply the background of unfaltering love and acceptance from which the client draws the strength he needs to grow again. It is not enough to put on this love and acceptance as a kind of surgeon's mask, a technique of treatment. It must be genuine. The pastor must be truly concerned with the sufferer and for the sufferer's own sake. Too often pastors appear as professional sympathizers and comforters. The troubled in mind, without quite knowing why, are usually repelled by such treatment. I do not mean that the pastor is necessarily hypocritical or without feeling. But sympathy is not enough. Empathy is needed. Empathy is to enter into another person's feelings, to live in them, to understand the other from within rather than from without, and yet while doing this to carry into the identification his own strength and maturity. It is by empathy that the knowledge of love and acceptance, and with them the sense of forgiveness, is conveyed and the strength is given to face the inner fears.

Where and how the pastor can get this capacity for empathy, the love and acceptance his client needs, will be considered more fully at a later point (see Chapter 10). However it comes to him it is not something external to him, something he can put on or take off at will. It is integral to his very self, an expression of what he has become as a person. It is encounter with a living person that the client needs, a person who is able by living with him in his inmost self to give him the right and the power to claim personality for himself. Method, technique, are important as disciplines of relationship but they can only be effective where a true meeting of persons has been achieved.

It is not enough to recognize the danger of relying on technique alone. A warning has to be given on the other side. The troubled client needs to encounter a person, but that person is not just the particularity of the pastor, his tastes, his temperament, his history, his foibles. These will all be there but they should be irrelevant. It is difficult to find words to describe what he needs to meet. Perhaps we may call it the outreach of a whole personality towards him, an outreach not to possess him, nor to restrain him, nor to drive him, but to give him the knowledge that he is worth while, that he is valuable because valued, lovable because loved. The pastor offers something much vaster than his own particularity. He offers meaning and value in life. I would say he offers God. This has to be explained in a later chapter. But the significant point is that the client does not take it from him; he finds it in himself. This is the peculiarity of a true personal encounter. There are no impersonal words to describe it. It is a special mode of the mutual immanence which characterizes all personal being.

5

Problems from Later Infancy

Somewhere about the age of two a remarkable thing happens to the infant. Where before he was conscious, that is, his mind was working, he now becomes self-conscious, aware of himself as having experiences and aware of an object beyond himself, beyond his mind, which he is seeing, touching, hearing, and so on. He does not perceive this world beyond himself as an adult sees it, ordered and arranged into identifiable objects in three dimensional spatial relationships and with sight and sound and kinaesthetic sensations co-ordinated. It is still largely a blur of sensations with a pattern at the heart of it, his mother. She has been involved in almost all his most vivid experiences. She is at first the meaning of the world to him. When he becomes self-conscious the unity of mother-and-baby, which marks early infancy, divides into two, and the infant is cut off, as it were, from the world in which he is set, by the recognition of self and not-self. Of course there remain many areas in which the line of division has still to be drawn and probably it is never completed even in adult years, for we know how difficult it is to observe distinctions in non-familiar areas of experience—sheep in a flock all look alike to the non-shepherd—and how easy it is to be deceived by appearances. In severe cases of disorder we project outside ourselves hallucinations originating in our own minds and perceive them as part of objective reality.

Nevertheless, although the distinction between self and not-self, between infant and mother in the first place and later between self and the world of objects and people, is never fully drawn, the realization of selfhood is a tremendous step forward. It lifts personal relations on to a new level, gives them a new dimension. It is at a considerable cost. In the first place we are henceforth shut up in the prison of our own individuality. Solitariness becomes our lot. There is no logical proof that the world we perceive is more than the creation of our own minds, the stuff of dreams. We can argue a case that it is overwhelmingly probable that the objective world does exist, but in the end we accept it by faith, or by habit, or because if we doubt its real existence we destroy any meaning in our own existence and meaning is essential to our inner sanity, which depends upon coherence.

Occasionally we encounter individuals who have lost this faith in the actuality of the beyond-self. While this state lasts they suffer great disorientation and confusion and are tormented by loneliness, dread, and aimlessness of purpose. It usually occurs in adolescents or young adults and perhaps in those of an intellectual disposition. This state differs from the sense of non-being described in the previous chapter. In that the world is real enough; it is the ego which doubts its own existence. In the solipsistic state which I am now describing the self is real, the world a realm of shadows. The sense of belonging with the world, the sense of community, of intimacy, of immanence, has disappeared. The break from the mother has probably been too sharp and the relations on the higher self-conscious level not firmly enough established, so the self is unable to accept the world in its new richness, yet, having reached self-consciousness, cannot relapse into the pre-personal stage of before self-consciousness. These are severe cases. We all experience, early or late, that vivid moment when we say to ourselves, "I am myself" and usually go on to add, with a feeling of loss, "and I can never know what it is like to be someone else"—the converse of

> Oh wad some power the giftie gie us
> To see oursels as others see us.

Clients who are suffering from this loss of belief in the reality of the world do not need argument to prove the world really exists. They are not the victims of intellectual solipsism but of the existential or relational kind. They need to feel the impact of the world upon them in love and interest shown to them. Argument of a philosophical kind is less valuable for the content of the argument than for the interest in the sufferer which willingness to argue reveals. They need the opportunity to talk about their doubts and to learn that others have had the same experience and can understand what they are talking about: that it is the common lot of mankind. They need to be led on to see that it is the pre-condition of man becoming the spear point of evolution. But it is not merely the intellectual understanding of this that is required. It is man's lot that to be man he has to accept the responsibilities, the burdens, and the anguish of being an individual. He has to discover through the experience of living and growing that he can only be an individual and fully himself in a context of other people similar to himself, that his solitariness does not cut him off completely from other people but if fully accepted enriches his relations with them. The solipsist finds it hard to reach out by his own initiative, except for the cry for help, towards other people, so he needs to feel that the pastor and the loving community are reaching out to him.

The attainment of self-consciousness is more frequently accompanied by another failure of development which is far more commonly encountered in counselling and more widespread in its effects. It also figures largely in cases of neurotic disorder which more properly come under the care of psychotherapists as severe separation anxiety. In this form it is the inability to tolerate the loss of the mother. We have already seen that for the health of the infant the mother has to help him endure deprivation, frustration, discomfort, and loneliness in the measure that his growing ego can bear it, to learn to wait for richer satisfactions. If in the earlier period overgreat strains have been put upon him he will find it hard to bear the separation from his mother when, coming to self-consciousness himself, he recognizes her as a person apart from himself. The division becomes a loss instead of a forward step to richer relations with her. The fear of losing her or the pain at having lost her drive him to regression. He will try to go back to the times when he was in full unity with her. He cannot bear the separation; he cannot move forward. Move forward he must, for life drives him onward, so his desire to remain in the earlier period of unity is repressed and remains with him as a constant powerful but unconscious motive. As he grows this will enter into all his relationships. He will long for security and be afraid of the future and the unknown. He will hark back to the good old days. He will suffer from loneliness and a longing for the past. In his dreams and fantasies he will re-visit the scenes of his childhood and will always be liable to nostalgia. He will be reluctant to make changes and may find it painful to make his departure from social gatherings or to say goodbye even to new acquaintances. Separation and aloneness revive the feelings of losing his mother in whom he found full relatedness and the sense of being a person. The extent and depth of this feeling is witnessed by the universal legend of a Golden Age in the past. It enters deeply into religion, as I have described elsewhere,[1] in the pictures of a heaven which is clearly the restoration of the lost unity with the mother, a return to the womb or to the blissful experience of having every pleasure given to us without effort.

The quest of the lost mother permeates the whole of human civilization in one form or another, both healthy and unhealthy, sublimated or repressed, mature or infantile. It is too vast a subject to pursue in detail here. So far as pastoral care is concerned it is enough to note that it is those who have been caught in the infantile forms who will be likely to seek the help of the pastor, particularly when the lost mother motive has entered into the conflicts of the

[1] Cf. *Freud and Christianity.*

Oedipus Complex period to which we shall turn in a moment. We shall see that it then takes the form of fixation in infantile love for the mother, leading to serious difficulties in love relationships. But in all cases involving the struggle to recapture the lost mother the pastor should realize that is is a fantasy mother that is being sought. The Church and its consolations, like the conventional ideas of heaven, may become by substitution such a mother and clinging to her may easily be mistaken for true devotion. The temptation to ministers of religion is to encourage dependence on the Church, since outwardly at least it appears as a witness to his successful ministry to have a congregation who centre their lives upon the church and its services. Without going more deeply into it we may say that this mistakes the mission of the Church, which is to send its members into the world to proclaim and live their faith there. The fantasy mother who is found in the Church—and elsewhere, of course—is the pre-separation mother, the mother of early infancy, the mother to whom we try to return when we cannot bear the strains which come from realization of our separateness. Hence in trying to help those who are running back to mother to avoid independence and responsibility, the pastor will not try to provide this fantasy mother either in his church or in his own person. Instead he will try to be a replacement for the real mother, with whom, for whatever reason, relations failed. That is, he will try to carry his client forward to independence by enabling him to grow again in an atmosphere of love and faith in him. In such an atmosphere, or relationship, the client feels able to assert himself more easily and fears failure less, for the pastor does not threaten explicitly or appear implicitly to withdraw his love if the client follows his normal promptings and begins to make decisions of his own accord. It is to this assumption of responsibility, which may appear to be rejection of the pastor, or of his advice, or criticism of the Church and its teachings, to which the pastor will seek to lead him.

Let us now turn to the great problem of later infancy, the

effects of the Oedipus Complex. The magnitude of the problem is shown by the fact that almost all of Freud's extensive writings are concerned with the Oedipus Complex, its origins, and its consequences. It is only possible here to indicate the main lines of development or failure of development, and it must be left to the pastor to recognize variations of them when he meets them in his work. But first we must note that two distinctions have to be drawn. The first of these is in the different ways that the boy and the girl enter into and get fixed in or pass successfully through this stage. We shall follow the development of the boy.[1] The second distinction is between healthy development and mal-development, that is, the failure to grow through the Oedipus Complex. Let us first take the healthy, or normal, development.

The Oedipus Complex is the complex of pressures which develops in the boy as the result of his growth. Having attained self-consciousness and the knowledge that his mother stands over against him as a separate person he very soon distinguishes other persons in his environment, particularly his father. His world, while growing clearer, is at the same time growing more complicated and he becomes involved in inner conflicts. Three major elements are involved in them. First of all his normal growth has brought changes in the functioning of his sex instincts. He has passed through the oral and anal stages into the phallic and it is now his penis which is the chief organ of interest and sensuous excitation. Secondly, his love for his mother which dominated his first two years continues, but now tends to focus in his sexual organs. Thirdly, there is his attitude towards his father. This is ambivalent. On the one hand he sees his father as all-powerful and omniscient, as a being to be admired as well as loved, and he longs to be like his father. He identifies himself with his father, that is, he tries

[1] For the feminine line of development see R. S. Lee, *Your Growing Child and Religion*, Chapters 6 and 7.

to live in his father, to think and feel and act like him so that he may become what he is. This is an unconscious or involuntary process, not like imitation, which is usually deliberate. On the other hand, he soon sees that his father has some power over his mother and takes her from him. He is too undeveloped to be able to understand that his mother loves his father, for he is inevitably egotistic and at this stage he can only grasp love that is directed towards himself. His love for his mother dominates him, therefore he imagines that her love for him is what she lives for. After all, his experience of her has shown this to him. The father therefore appears as a rival who will take his mother from him, and a dangerous rival since he is so large and all-powerful. The boy is caught between his desire to have his mother and his fear of his father. This is the main line of the Oepidus Complex. He wants to get rid of his father to retain undisputed enjoyment of his mother. Inevitably he projects his destructive desire on to his father and fears that the latter will get rid of him. Chiefly he fears that his father will destroy his capacity to love the mother. As at this stage his sensuous longings and fantasies have become associated with his penis he fears that his father will cut it off, that is, will castrate him.

The Oedipus Complex is a normal development and serves an essential function in the mental growth of the young child. The relative strength of the forces at work in it in any given individual depends upon his particular constitution and the circumstances of his upbringing. For instance he has already suffered losses analogous to castration. To be born, thrust out of the comfort of the womb, was such an experience. And in his weaning he lost the beloved breast finally, after having had it taken from him many times before. Further, in self-awareness of his own individuality he lost the intimacy of possessing the mother and had to surrender her to the world beyond himself. Many other factors can influence the strength of the different urges in him, particularly behaviour on the part of his parents that is too variable.

The normal outcome of the Oedipus Complex is an interesting one for its significance for the structure of the developing mind of the infant. The little boy is caught between incompatible drives, the urge to live, to save himself, and his desire for his mother which will bring him sure destruction at the hands of the father. If he persists in his wish to possess his mother in a sensual (sexual) way he will have to pay the penalty. His self-love or narcissism wins, but not by a straightforward trial of strength. He reinforces his fear of the father and his desire to live by identifying himself with the father. He takes his father into himself, as it were, and gives the orders to himself that he thinks his father is giving. He is able to do this not just because he is afraid of the father but because one part of him sees the father as the ideal he wishes to become. He is thus enabled to renounce his sensual desire of the mother. His love for her turns into affection. She becomes an "aim-inhibited" love-object.

The image of the father which the boy has taken into his mind becomes a permanent part of the structure of it. This is what we know as the "super-ego". It carries with it all the commands which the boy supposed the father (and the mother) were giving him and it becomes the repository of all subsequent rules of conduct accepted by him. It is the seat of his moral conscience because, through its being internalized and made part of his mind, its functioning means that he is giving orders to himself. He has made it authoritative over his conduct, the watchdog over what is forbidden as wrong, and he feels obliged to obey it. As he grows, the rules which it enforces should develop with his greater experience and to meet the wider demands that society will make upon him.[1]

The abnormal outcome of the Oedipus Complex is where it is not resolved satisfactorily in this way. There may be many reasons for it. Usually the chief reason is abnormal

[1] See Note 2 at the end of this chapter.

attachment to the mother because the infant has been over-stimulated sensually and emotionally, or to a fantasy of the mother as we saw earlier in this chapter. The stronger the feeling for the mother the stronger is the fear of the father. In that case it is harder for the boy to make a positive identification with his father and take him into his mind as a healthy control over his desires. Instead he holds on in his fantasies to his mother and also in his fantasies accepts the penalty, castration. He represses his mother fixation and his castration into his unconscious and projects his fear of the father on to every authority figure. He is fixed in some measure in his Oedipus Complex. One consequence of this, if the fixation is severe, is to render him liable to psychosomatic illness—anxiety, hysteria, obsessions, phobias, etc.—which require psychotherapy. In less severe cases the fixation will manifest itself in character traits and in periods of tension under various stresses. There are likely to be marriage problems, because every woman is likely to be seen under some aspect of his unconscious fixation on his mother and the veto imposed by the image of the dreaded father. In his unconscious, because he has not given up his mother, he has accepted castration. Superficially, this will reveal itself also in what is commonly called an inferiority complex. Further, because he has not resolved his feelings towards his father he may alternate between subservience to authority figures and defiance and rebellion towards them. In most cases some authority figures are given obedience, while others are defied. The acceptance and rebellion are also likely to be extended beyond persons to institutions and systems of thought and conduct.

The range of the operation of the Oedipus Complex is so vast, witness Freud's work, that it is futile to try to alert the pastor to what he may encounter. It will take many forms in the people who come to him for help. He needs, however, to remember two things: first, that it is normal to enter the Oedipus Complex—it is disastrous not to do so—and the healthy pass through it; and, secondly, behind fixation in it there almost certainly lie earlier traumas which pre-disposed to fixation. The theory of the Oedipus Complex is fairly easy to grasp and for that reason pastors may be tempted to air their knowledge with their clients when they recognize that this lies at the root of their troubles. To do so would of course be a blunder, for it would be to usurp the function of analyst, for which they are not trained. It so happens that psychotherapy is more effective with cases rooted in the Oedipus Complex than in any other area, for it is here that the severe repressions leading to the psychoneuroses take their origin. Other illnesses, which are disorders of the structure of the personality and belong to the earlier period of infancy, are not so amenable to analysis. They are psychotic in nature. Strangely enough these open a field of opportunity for pastoral care. Addressing the Association of Social Workers, London, Dr D. W. Winnicott said, "Psychoneurotic illness can be severe indeed. Moreover, this type of illness makes the social worker despair, because the repressed unconscious is the province of the psychoanalyst. By contrast— the areas of illness named psychosis, or madness, offer more scope for the social worker, and this partly because such disorders offer less scope for the psychoanalyst, unless, indeed, he steps outside his role at appropriate moments and himself becomes a social worker." He explains this in these terms: "I think of each social worker as a therapist, but not as the kind of therapist who makes the correct and well-timed interpretation that elucidates the transference neuroses. Do this if you like, but your more important function is therapy of the kind that is always being carried on by parents in correction of relative failures in environmental provision. What do such parents do? They exaggerate some parental function and keep it up for a length of time, in fact until the child has used it up and is ready to be released from special care."[1]

[1] Dr D. W. Winnicott, *The Maturational Processes and the Facilitating Environment*, pp. 219 and 227.

Dr Winnicott is here addressing trained professional social workers, particularly those who have the care of children. In their own way clergy are also professional social workers, but unfortunately they are not as yet adequately trained in the principles of casework, although that is being remedied to some extent and it is the aim of this little book to suggest the principles both of the work and of the kind of training which they should be given. His remarks therefore apply to pastoral care with some adaptations. Social caseworkers in general have their cases referred to them from various official or semi-official sources. Some cases will be referred to the pastor but usually they will come to him direct or he will encounter them in the course of his normal work. Further, social caseworkers have official authority with the sanction of the law standing behind them. The pastor, on the other hand, has only the moral authority of his office behind him. But with both the success of their work will depend on the skill with which they carry it out and the strength of the personal relations they are able to establish with their clients. In both the essential function is to be good parent replacements to enable their clients to recover from the ill effects of bad parent relations in an earlier period. Social caseworkers may be dealing with children in need of care, as Dr Winnicott's words imply, but the pastor, though he will also at times be involved with children, will mostly have adults to care for and counsel. Yet, as I have said earlier, the principle remains. Part of the personality of the client seeking help is always the infant in him that has been unable to grow, so he will inevitably in that respect take a childish attitude to the pastor. The latter's problem is to disentangle the infantile from the adult in his client's behaviour so as to strengthen the adult and foster the abandonment of the infantile attitudes. His task may be more complicated than that of the caseworker. On the other hand, as we shall see at a later point, his vocation should give him greater resources.

There is a further distinction emerging from what Dr

Winnicott says. He is talking about severe cases both of psycho-neurosis and of psychosis, which he designates as madness, I think for the simple purpose of emphasizing his point to his listeners. Undoubtedly the pastor will encounter many such cases. But the greater part of his work will be with people who at first sight at least do not need the attentions of a psychiatrist or analyst. Of course the pastor cannot be certain. His function is not diagnosis. For his own sake he must be on the alert to recognize the significance of symptoms he may encounter so that he may call in the help of a psychiatrist where it seems advisable. Where it can be arranged he should always work in co-operation with doctors and psychiatrists so that whenever anything doubtful appears he may be able to refer to the expert. His expertise is not in diagnosis but is, or should be, in personal relations. Between the severe cases and normal healthiness lies a broad spectrum of cases seemingly, and in most instances actually, not in need of psychotherapeutic care yet unable to manage their lives successfully or tormented by doubts and fears. Some of these will be of the psycho-neurotic type, that is, suffering from repressions related to the Oedipus Complex conflicts. Others will be of the psychotic type, suffering from inadequate development of personality, deriving from factors operating in the pre-oedipal period. Usually there will be a mixture of both.

The pastor as such has not had the necessary training to diagnose what is neurotic and what psychotic in his client, nor is it necessary for him to do so to perform his therapeutic function. He needs, as I have said, to be on the alert for symptoms which warn him that he should call in the help of a psychotherapist, and he must also be prepared for the persistence of some of the troubles of his client, even when these appear to be minor ones. These are the ones that make "the social worker despair". They may be troublesome but not so incommoding to the sufferer that they warrant the time, expense, and effort involved in taking them to a psychotherapist. It often is better to induce the client to accept them as a permanent handicap and in so doing to divest them of some of their emotional significance, much as smoking is a relatively harmless neurotic outlet—unless carried to the extremes that bring the risk of lung cancer. Instead, therefore, of classifying his clients into neurotic and psychotic, the pastor will treat each of them as an individual person in need of his help and establish with each the healing personal relationship which it is within his power to give and which is his function as pastor.

NOTE 1

PHYSICAL CAUSATION AND TREATMENT OF MENTAL ILLNESS

No reference has been made above to the physical or somatic causes of mental disease. It is well known that certain diseases, and old age, lead to deterioration of the nervous system, thereby hindering the functioning of the mind. There is considerable evidence to suggest that some at least of the personality disorders of the psychotic type may be caused by biochemical factors, deficiency or excess of substances produced by the body, making the brain an inefficient organ. Various physical remedies, tranquillizers, anti-depressants, and so on, have been brought into use with varying success with such disorders. The administration of these must be entirely the province of doctors and particularly psychiatrists. The discovery and use of these has been entirely empirical; the biochemical causes of mental disorder have not been discovered. Research goes on constantly and it is to be hoped that there may be greater insight gained into causes and cure.

All this, however, does not affect what has been said above. Man is a psychosomatic being; that is, he is both body and mind. We cannot explain how the two are interrelated and bodily processes are transformed into mental events. It seems quite clear that body influences mind and mind body by some kind of interaction. Both are involved in every human action. We may look on the brain as the co-ordinating and connecting instrument through which the impulses from either side are conveyed to the other. If for biochemical reasons the brain is impaired the mind cannot function properly, just as a blow on the head may lead to unconsciousness. Conversely, in conversion hysteria mental aims are expressed in physical forms, functional paralysis, blindness, and so on. But the mind tries to function against the handicap of the mal-functioning brain; it tries to integrate experiences, to develop personality, to adjust to the world outside the self. What psychological help can be given is all the more needed to support this struggle to grow. This support is what the pastor can give.

NOTE 2

THE STRUCTURE OF THE MIND

For an understanding of some of the common problems which are met in counselling, especially those which involve feelings of guilt or raise matters of sin and morals, it is very important to have a clear grasp of the structure of the mind which is developed as the individual grows and which is summed up in the psychoanalytic theory of the id, ego, and super-ego. The classic formulation of this is to be found in Freud's work, *The Ego and the Id*. Simpler expositions are to be had in R. S. Lee's *Your Growing Child and Religion* and *Freud and Christianity*, both of which may be obtained in Penguin editions.

Putting it in the most general terms we may describe the id as the primary self, the basic source of all the energies of the mind, the seat of desire, containing some pre-formed, inherited patterns of outlet which we know as instincts, but which are far more plastic and modifiable by experience in man than in the lower animals. When contact with the world begins consciousness takes over and adjusts the demands of the id to reality, in the light of knowledge gained by experience. This accumulation of knowledge and the resultant direction of the id is the work of the ego. The ego uses consciousness as its tool. The ego is thus a modification of the id and its aim is to procure from the world the satisfactions which the needs of the id demand. One of its functions is to recognize danger situations and to safeguard the self. Such a situation springs up in the Oedipus Complex period and, as we have seen, the ego is torn between the imperative desires of the id and the (apparent) overwhelming threat of destruction. The result of this, in the normal resolution of the Oedipus Complex, is a modification in turn of the ego, by which is set up a super-ego as a permanent part of the self, whose function is to impose standards of conduct among which are moral laws or principles. The id, ego, and super-ego working together constitute the whole self or personality.

Since this complex structure of the self only occurs as the result of development in the early years of life and in reaction to the social environment of the child, his family, it is obvious that the balances between the three functions will vary with each individual. Further, it is always likely that the development will not go through smoothly; the ego may be too weak, the super-ego too strong. Or some fail to develop an adequate super-ego and become psychopathic. Or, again, circumstances may lead to fixation in the patterns of satisfaction established in infancy, even though they are not appropriate to adult life.

For healthy life it is desirable that the ego should be the dominant function, but without the id it would have no motive for action, and without the guidance of the super-ego would not be able to adjust to other people. One of the aims of pastoral counselling must be to enable the client to develop a strong ego.

6

The Work of Pastoral Care

If we were studying the normal development of man we would go on now to consider how his mind expands in childhood (6–12 years) and the later stages, and indeed it is important to have this knowledge. We are concerned, however, with how to help people who have personal problems. It is true that in adolescence and old age problems come in the normal course of development but these can be considered separately. Those problems of course can be accentuated by some breakdown of growth in the infantile period but, in so far as they do, they belong to the groups that we have been considering. Instead, therefore, of going on to discuss childhood and its contribution we turn now to examine how the pastor goes about the work of pastoral care of his clients.

Let me summarize the basic nature of the disorders which he will be asked to help. The new-born child is possessed of an innate urge to life and growth. This displays itself in three aspects. First, he has to integrate his experience so that he brings order into the chaos of sensations which are the raw material of his mind. By integration he comes to perceive a world of objects and events co-ordinated in space and time and at the same time unifies, so far as he is able, his own inner life of impulses, felt needs, satisfactions, pains, and so on. This leads him on to the second aspect, the formation of his personality, separating him from the world he experiences and at the same time opening the way to more complex and richer relations with that world, particularly with other persons. He should achieve a self-identity. This is only completed after adolescence, but the infant has to attain the first basic stages. Thirdly, he has to become reality-adapted, object-related, accepting the objective world as the area of his living instead of retreating from it into the fantasy world of his wishes. Towards the end of infancy the strength of his wishes and the perception of dangers in the outside world bring him to a profound experience (the resolution of the Oedipus Complex) which results in the alteration of the structure of his personality by the formation of the super-ego, which gives him an interior instrument for self-control and also brings a new dimension into his relations with the outside world.

In any of the character deformations, or psychoses, there is some failure belonging to early infancy and it is bound to show itself in weaknesses of all three aspects of growth. In the psychoneuroses, severe or mild, the client is subjected to a double conflict. First, there is an unresolved conflict from the Oedipus Complex stage which has been repressed into the unconscious where its activity creates a permanent weakness; and, second, a stress situation occurs, such as, for instance, marriage or over-dominant superiors, which bears upon the weaknesses and forces the client to retreat into illness to protect himself from the pressure. A later stress situation is not enough in itself to cause a breakdown; there must always be a preceding failure in infancy to establish the underlying weakness. Anyone who has successfully negotiated infancy has the strength to adjust himself to later stresses. Hence the importance of infancy.

The psychoanalyst is able in the course of analysis to take his patient back into the period of infancy and unveil the repressed conflict, so that he can grow through it in the favourable situation of the analysis and get the strength to face and deal with the current stress. The pastor cannot do this. He meets his client in his present conflict. Because the client is not so severely incapacitated as to need the help of psychoanalysis, his infantile weakness may not be so great as in the cases of severe breakdown, and the pastor can give some help. He needs to remember, however, that there is an infantile root to the trouble and that his client will be behaving in infantile ways towards him even when he presents his problem in adult terms.

What then can he do? How does he react to his client and behave towards him? We cannot do better than reflect over the description of their work given in the address referred to in the previous chapter delivered by Dr Winnicott to the Association of Caseworkers.[1] He ends by saying:

What you find yourself providing in your work can be described in the following ways:

You apply yourself to the case.

You get to know what it feels like to be your client.

You become *reliable* for the limited field of your professional responsibility.

You behave yourself professionally.

You concern yourself with your client's problem.

You accept being in the position of a subjective object in the client's life, while at the same time you keep both your feet on the ground.

You accept love, and even the in-love state, without flinching and without acting-out your response.

You accept hate, and meet it with strength rather than with revenge.

You tolerate your client's illogicality, unreliability, suspicion, muddle, fecklessness, meanness, etc., etc., and recognize all these unpleasantnesses as symptoms of distress. (In private life these same things would make you keep at a distance.)

You are not frightened, nor do you become overcome when your client goes mad, disintegrates, runs out in the street in a nightdress, attempts suicide and perhaps succeeds. If murder threatens you call in the police to help not only yourself but also the client. In all these emergencies you recognize the client's call for help, or a cry of despair because of loss of hope of help.

In all these respects you are, in your limited professional area, a person deeply involved in feeling, yet at the same time detached in that you know that you have no responsibility for

[1] Op. cit., p. 229.

the fact of your client's illness, and you know the limits of your powers to alter a crisis situation. If you can hold the situation together the possibility is that the crisis will resolve itself, and then it will be because of you that a result will be achieved.

This advice given by Dr Winnicott applies, with very little adaptation, to the work of pastoral care, so I shall take his points one by one and comment on them with that in mind.

You apply yourself to the case.

Social workers usually have their cases referred to them by various authorities. In pastoral work relatives or friends often ask the pastor to give his help to someone in need, or his doctor may invite the pastor's co-operation, but the greater number of people come direct to him. He may or may not know them beforehand. His first duty is to treat the case seriously, that is, to give his full attention to it, to listen carefully to what is said to him, however trivial or improbable the story may be. The client is in need of help. The nature of the help needed may not be obvious at first sight and the client may be mistaken about what he really needs, for much of his trouble will be in his unconscious mind. He does not really know why he has come to the pastor and when he begins to speak he is very apologetic about taking up his time and how good the pastor is to see him and he finds it difficult to explain his troubles. He is in a state of conflict. Because his root trouble is unconscious he is unable to say directly what it is; but because it is trouble, his coming is a plea for help. The pastor has to discover what the real trouble is and, more important, help the client to gain the insight into himself necessary to recognize the trouble, and he cannot do this unless he gives undivided attention to what is said to him. What is said, and also what is not said but might be expected to be said, is likely to give a clue to the hidden problem.

You get to know what it feels like to be your client.

This is probably the most important single element in the success of pastoral care. It is also the most difficult. It is easy enough to feel sympathy for someone in trouble, to desire to help them, to share and relieve them of their anxieties and fears. To get inside them and live in them, to feel the tensions tearing them apart, to experience the reality of their fears, that is, to have empathy with them, is much more difficult. It requires understanding and it demands an identification with them which enables the pastor to think and feel with his client while at the same time retaining his own identity. In "non-directive" counselling, associated with the name of Carl Rogers,[1] the counsellor "reflects" as in a mirror the thoughts and emotions of his client, enabling him to see himself more clearly. The counsellor does not explain to the client what he is saying, though he tries to restate it in the simplest and clearest form so as to help the client understand himself. Still less does he attempt to instruct the client what he ought to think and feel. By simply reflecting the mind of the client the pastor is doing something more than letting the client understand himself; he is, in the eyes of the latter, accepting him, giving him full permission to be what he is. He is thus reducing the fear of the client that he is unlovable and this makes it easier for the client to accept himself instead of fighting against what he has kept in his unconscious and refused to face. The pastor can do this only in so far as he is able to get inside the other, become him for the time being, yet in doing so he must remain the pastor to whom the client is trying to reveal himself. At times the client will try to take up a dependent role, asking openly by what he says or implicitly by his attitude for the pastor to advise him, give him instructions, take responsibility for his actions, make decisions for him. He is trying to manipulate him. This demand too the pastor must reflect and bring

[1] *Counselling and Psychotherapy* and *Client-Centered Therapy*.

into the open, but without condemnation and without
accepting the role that is being thrust upon him.

There are few temptations harder for the pastor to resist
than that of being an instructor and adviser to his client. His
office as minister of religion is one of authority. In some of
his work it is his duty to teach, advise, and instruct, and he
may have already done so to the person who now comes as a
client seeking help with his emotional problems, that is,
those stemming from emotional conflicts. But in this situation he should not drop into the authority role. By his
empathy with the client he will know the feeling of need for
advice and direction to be strong and sincere, even if swollen
by unconscious motives, and his sympathy for the client may
press him to try to give the help that is asked for, but this
will mean that he loses sight of what his function in the
pastoral care situation is, namely, to help the client to grow
and become himself, integrated and mature. It is therefore
his task to remain himself even while he enters into the feelings of the client. If the latter is able to manipulate him the
pastor has lessened the chance of being able to give lasting
help, and instead has confirmed his client in his infantile
attitudes.

You become reliable *for the limited field
of your professional responsibility.*

Social caseworkers, such as psychiatric social workers, medical social workers, children's officers, probation officers, have
clearly defined fields of work and responsibility. Some of
the duties of the clergy are also clearly defined, such as the
conduct of worship, instruction in the faith, and so on, but
their responsibility for those committed to their care is to
all intents and purposes unlimited. There is no aspect of
life which is not the concern of religion, but because this is
so it is impossible to define the form of responsibility which
the clergy hold and many different conceptions of what it is
are to be found in practice. Nevertheless the pastor must try

to arrive at some conception of what his general office entails. This book is an attempt to describe what is involved in one section of his work and by what means he can carry it out most successfully, but this needs to be reconciled with the rest of his work. There are many clergy who hold an authoritarian view of their office, for carefully thought out reasons and not because they are immature and unconsciously try to bolster up their inner weaknesses by adopting authoritarian attitudes; and these argue that counselling, even in the limited sense in which I have described it under the name of pastoral care, by the non-directive client-centred methods I am advocating, is a practical impossibility to the parish priest, because he is involved with his people in many other ways where he is directive. Because he cannot divest himself of his general office, in the eyes of his client at least, and remains the same person, he cannot be both directive and non-directive. Clergy holding these views may believe in the value of pastoral counselling but argue that it should be carried out by specialist pastors without parochial responsibilities.

This is a legitimate point of view to maintain. I do not think it is satisfactory or goes deep enough, for reasons I hope to make clearer in a later chapter.[1] Here I am only concerned to insist that the pastor must continually ask himself what is his responsibility towards his client and must also integrate the answer he arrives at with the interpretation of his other responsibilities. It is very easy to deceive oneself with glib answers. If he believes himself to be "a father in God" to his people, on what model does he pattern his fatherhood? If "God's chosen representative ('by the grace of God')", what kind of a God does he represent? So we may go on. Basically the pastor needs to be able to answer the question "What am I trying to do with my client?" The answer can only be given in terms of his conception of God and man and of how God works in man and in the

[1] See Chapter 10.

world. I suggest that we may think of his task as ministering the love of God (and his wisdom) to the client, by loving him as God loves him. If it is his responsibility to do this he must be "reliable" in it. He cannot swing between love and not-love with different people or with the same person at different times. Like God he must show "no shadow of turning".

You behave yourself professionally.
You concern yourself with your client's problem.

We can take these two directives together. To behave professionally means two things for the pastor. He must try to the best of his ability to give the help which his client has asked for by coming to see him, and he must respect the rights of other people who may be involved with him, probation officers, for instance.

A pastor has many calls upon his time and attention and in English conditions he does not usually have an office at the church where he may be interviewed between certain hours but generally sees people in his study at home. He is liable to all sorts of interruptions and sometimes may be tempted to feel that his client's troubles as he has stated them are trivial and his fears groundless. To dismiss them lightly would be most unprofessional. The client is afraid of his own problem and almost certainly cannot say what his real trouble is; part of the pastoral work is to bring this into the light. Behind the triviality which is expressed may lie something quite serious. He must be listened to with serious attention. This means that time must be given to him. The "couple of minutes" he asks for is likely to stretch to an hour. If the time is not available when he comes he should be heard briefly and another visit arranged when the pastor is not so pressed. He concerns himself with his client. That means concerning himself with the client's problem, but as pastor he is more responsible for the well-being of the client as a person than are other case-workers. He meets him in and through his problems. The first encounter is only a beginning of the relationship but it gives the pastor the opportunity of showing that the client is important to him. Without this the relationship cannot grow and help is impossible. But again the warning must be given that the pastor must feel this importance. He cannot put on as a professional technique the manner of loving the client, of being interested in his welfare, of desiring to help him, and hope to deceive him. He must be sincere in his concern or the client will sense the insincerity and be discouraged. There is nothing so repellent as mere "professional" heartiness. Counselling requires strength in the counsellor before all else.

It frequently happens that the client is already involved with someone else, psychiatrist, general practitioner, probation officer, social caseworker, before coming to the pastor, or may have to be referred by the latter to one of these. They have their professional responsibilities towards him and the pastor must respect these and work with whoever else is involved with his client. Differences of opinion are bound to arise, for instance between doctor and pastor over whether a dying person should be told that he is dying, and who has the over-riding right of decision. There is no final answer to this. It is better, since all are concerned with the welfare of the client, to try to work out an *ad hoc* solution. Such clashes are less likely to happen if the pastor makes a habit of co-operating regularly with other caseworkers.

You accept being in the position of a subjective object in the client's life, while at the same time you keep both your feet on the ground.

This is one of the most demanding aspects of pastoral care. The pastor, because he is inevitably an authority figure, will encounter it in all his work, and though it is intensified in situations calling for counselling the fact that the client seeks help gives an opportunity of overcoming it. The pastor should always be on the watch for it so that he may understand the true nature of the client's behaviour.

The client is unable to view the pastor objectively and interpret his motives, action, and character as they really are. He is under the domination of his unconscious attitudes or the distortions which accompany deformed development of personality. In particular he projects on to him father (or mother) images belonging to his infantile unconscious and sees him in the light of these. He distorts what the pastor says and does to fit this subjective picture of him and is constantly seeking motives in him which are not there. He expects the pastor to behave like an over-indulgent or over-stern parent to infant, although the adult part of him may put forward apparently sound reasons for his attitudes. This can be very trying to the patience of the pastor. Argument about the validity of the reasons is ineffective because it does not touch the real ground of the misinterpretation. The pastor must in no circumstances lose patience. He must remember that the client cannot help his behaviour; it is part of his trouble. To blame him for it and utter recriminations is to decline to help. He must accept him as he is if he is to help him grow out of it. Therefore he must "keep both his feet on the ground", that is, stand firm in his position of being a good parent, loving and caring for his client without seeking to impose himself on him in any way at all, but only to help the client to find his true self.

You accept love, and even the in-love state, without flinching and without acting-out your response.

A patient undergoing analysis, as we have seen in an earlier chapter, develops a transference, that is, he transfers on to the analyst the attitudes which as an infant he took towards his parents, together with the emotions appropriate to them, attitudes and emotions which had been retained in his unconscious. In some measure there is transference in all human relations, but in the analytic situation it is greatly intensified.

In pastoral care transference will also develop strongly. This will result in the client loving and even falling in love with the pastor. The client as an infant was in love with his parents but his love could only be shown to them in an infantile way. The same love transferred in adulthood to the pastor is always likely to express itself in adult modes of sexuality. This can be potentially embarrassing to the pastor, but he must accept that it happens and recognize its trans-ference nature. If he responds to it by praise or blame as if it were entirely adult behaviour and allows his feelings to pass into action, he does harm to his client. On the one hand by responding to the sensual approaches he is preventing the client from learning the infantile nature of his feelings and may intensify the inner conflict, and on the other by condemning them he is rejecting the infant's love for his parents and confirming the infant's unconscious fear that he is unloved and unlovable. The love that he gives in response must be that of interest and concern for the client as a person in which sensuous behaviour has little place.

*You accept hate and meet it with strength
rather than with revenge.*

Perhaps "retaliation" is a better word here than "revenge". This is the obverse side of infantile feelings. The infant in one strand of his mind hates his parents. They, he feels, frustrate him, threaten him, deprive him, overpower him. He resents that he cannot always get at once what he desires and that he is forced to renounce or control some of his wishes. He hates his parents with infantile vigour, singly or together. Because the pastor becomes a parent figure he is likely to have this hate transferred to him. In this, too, he must recognize the infantile nature of the hate, accept it as normal to the situation and help his client to get insight into it also. If in any way he tries to retaliate by an answering hate or dislike, and by some form of punishment, he will only intensify the client's conflicts and fears. The pastor should realize that the hate has been repressed and has only been able to come into consciousness because the love shown by the pastor has given the client enough security to allow it to come out so far. The pastor is the safest person to hate because his love seems to be strong enough to bear the hate and so help the (buried) infant to get free of it. Retaliation destroys this possibility. So does moral condemnation of the hatred.

You tolerate your client's illogicality, unreliability, suspicion, muddle, fecklessness, meanness, etc., etc., and recognize all these unpleasantnesses, as symptoms of distress. (In private life these same things would make you keep at a distance.)

The picture Dr Winnicott draws here is not over-drawn. This is how people behave when they are in need of help and when they are being helped. It is essential for the pastor to recognize that such behaviour is really the symptom of trouble and not the trouble itself. The social caseworker does not have to take them on unless they are referred to him, so in his private life he can avoid people who behave in this way. For the pastor the matter is not so easy. He has some sort of responsibility for all his parishioners and he cannot simply avoid any of them who behave in this way. If they come to him for help his position is clear, he recognizes that they are sick people. But they may be, and probably are, just as sick if they do not come to him. In his assessment of them and in his day-to-day contacts with them he should bear this in mind and not reject them as worthless. If they are sick they are aware, unconsciously at least, of their need, and to be treated as worthless can only make them worse. The pastor, if he truly believes them not to be responsible for their behaviour, can show by his behaviour that he does not count *their* behaviour against them, that he understands and forgives. He needs infinite patience, but that is not enough; he needs interest in and love of people just because they are people.

Sometimes the pastor will find that a client he has started to help begins unexpectedly to behave in the way described. He should not be discouraged at this. It may be that through the new emotional security provided by the relationship with the pastor the client now feels free to bring out feelings which hitherto he had been unable to face and deal with, so the new behaviour is a sign of progress. Or it may be that he finds the warmth and trust offered him by the pastor so novel that he can scarcely believe it and he feels impelled to test its genuineness, like a little child who is deliberately naughty to test the extent to which his parents' love will go. The client will say something outrageous and watch the pastor (or counsellor) out of the corner of his eye to note his reactions. This, too, is a symptom of the underlying sickness, and needs to be received with loving patience and understanding.

You are not frightened, nor do you become overcome with guilt-feelings when your client goes mad, disintegrates, runs out in the street in a nightdress, attempts suicide and perhaps succeeds. If murder threatens, you call in the police to help not only yourself but also the client. In all these emergencies you recognize the client's call for help, or a cry of despair because of loss of hope of help.

The client is the pastor's responsibility and must be given all the help that it is in the pastor's power to give. This does not mean controlling his behaviour, taking charge of him, except in the rare and extreme cases where he threatens imminent danger to others or perhaps to himself. Talk of suicide is not necessarily such a threat. The pastor's responsibility is to give what help he can to foster growth to inner strength and greater maturity in his client and this requires the maximum freedom possible. In giving this he is relying on two things: the innate urge to health in his client, and the healing and creative power of love when it is of the non-possessive kind. Theologically this means that the pastor is relying on God's action, for God's action is not an alternative to the pastor's (plus other healing forces in the environment or within the client); it is the same thing seen under another aspect. The pastor is not all-powerful or omniscient. He may make mistakes. His failure may help him to see his mistakes and help him to do better in the future, but guilt-feelings cannot undo the failure. They only make him uncertain of himself and uncertain too of God. The pastor must have faith in the forces of life and having done all he can must wait calmly for what follows.

All this is summed up in Dr Winnicott's concluding paragraph:

In all these respects you are, in your limited professional area, a person deeply involved in feeling, yet at the same time detached in that you know that you have no responsibility for the fact of your client's illness, and you know the limits of your powers to alter a crisis situation. If you can hold the situation together the possibility is that the crisis will resolve itself, and then it will be because of you that a result is achieved.

In other words if you give the attention, love, trust, and understanding that the client needs, time is on your side. There is no magic formula which can procure instantaneously the growth by which alone healing can come.

7

The Pastor Himself

It should be clear from what has been said in previous chapters that the essential element in pastoral care/counselling work is the personal relationship established between the pastor and his client, by which the client is given a sense of emotional security and of his own value and is enabled to face his inner conflicts. The unequal character of the relationship has been described already. It concentrates on the welfare of the client. To reach its ideal development it requires that the pastor should make no demands for his own emotional satisfaction on the client beyond the pleasure that naturally comes from a mature relationship created with another person. He ought not to make unconscious demands upon the client. But this is an ideal situation and in actual fact we may anticipate that any pastor will have motives and aims of which he is unconscious and which will enter into the pastor–client relationship and hamper it to some extent. Part, therefore, of his training should be directed to freeing him from the damaging effect of his unconscious mind. If he is not freed, he will not be able to meet satisfactorily the demands from the unconscious mind of his client, for he will be blinded to the nature of many of these by his own unconscious.

Every psychoanalyst is expected to undergo a long and searching analysis as part of his training. It would be excellent if every pastor could be given analysis, but this is quite impracticable in present circumstances. I have urged that those who want to take up the more technical work of pastoral counselling should have analysis, but the best we can at present hope for those interested in general pastoral care is that their training should make them aware of the weaknesses to which they are liable and that they should have some training under adequate supervision in conducting interviews, training which will help them to recognize the trends of their own behaviour in the interview, to see in what ways they are imposing themselves upon the client and seeking satisfactions of their own. This training can only be given in actual practice in dealing with people. Here we can only point to some of the common attitudes which may be expected to show themselves to some extent operative in pastors. I shall consider the matter under four heads: the nature of the office, the motivation of candidates for the ministry, the effect of training in theological colleges, and the reactions to parish experience after ordination. This will open the way for some suggestions to improve training.

THE NATURE OF THE OFFICE

The office of minister of religion, pastor, is usually called a vocation. The meaning of this may range from implying an experience which is interpreted as a direct call from God to take up the office to the choice of it as a career which is rewarding in itself and not one made attractive because of the financial remuneration attaching to it. The stipends in fact offered are extremely low in comparison with other professions requiring equivalent standards of ability and training, so it can be assumed that the attractions of the office lie in the work it entails and in other satisfactions of a more subtle nature which are to be found in it. The core of it is the desire to serve God and man. The word minister means servant.

The work of the ministry falls into three divisions. First, the minister is called to "preach the gospel". That means to proclaim the historic acts of God as recorded in the scriptures. These require elucidation and interpretation, so immediately the work of preaching widens into teaching, not only from the pulpit but in every way that becomes available. The minister, too, needs to show the relevance of his theological preaching and teaching to the everyday life of the world. There is no limit to what preaching the gospel may entail.

Secondly, the office involves what the Anglican Church calls "the ministry of the sacraments". We can understand this in the widest sense to signify superintending the worship of God by his congregation, and this covers all the Churches. In some, less emphasis is placed on the use of sacraments in worship than in others, but all are agreed on the importance of worshipping together at frequent intervals.

Thirdly, the minister is charged with the responsibility of tending the flock committed to his charge, and from this the title "pastor" is derived. Part of the work as pastor is to carry out the first two duties faithfully, but beyond that he must as pastor concern himself with the needs of his people as individuals or small groups, in particular, families. Jesus charged his disciples to "heal the sick" and "tend my sheep". We recognize today that there is sickness of body, mind and spirit, that much that appears as evil is in reality sickness, and it is the pastoral function to heal the apparent sinner rather than to condemn him.

The minister is appointed to his office by the rules accepted by the Church to which he belongs and he thereby becomes an official of it with authority conferred on him by it. However sincerely he believes he is called by God to his work it is by means of the institution, the organized society which is the Church, that the calling is made effective. It is perhaps safer to say that we become ministers "by divine permission" rather than "by divine grace", except that God makes use of our failures and our sinfulness to turn them to good, though not necessarily in a way obvious to men. The important point for us to consider is that the minister by his appointment becomes an official or functionary of the Church which appoints him. In most Churches he is not merely in charge of his local congregation; he represents the wider Church to them and will have to act and speak on occasion on behalf of it. In doing so he carries behind him all the weight of history as well as the authority of the wider body. This weight and this authority are vested in him only because of his office, and do not belong to his character as an individual person, even though this is taken into account before he is placed in the office. As an official he is depersonalized. He becomes a representative, an agent. This is shown clearly in liturgical worship, which some would undoubtedly regard as the very heart of his duties. Sometimes he prays to God as speaking on behalf of his congregation, sometimes he speaks forgiveness or blessing to his people in the name of God, and his ceremonial attitudes may express this, when, for instance, he faces the altar or faces the congregation.

This functional role, if it is maintained as the essence of ministry, as it frequently is, comes into conflict with what is required of the minister in his work as pastoral care-counsellor. In this he cannot be an impersonal representative. It calls for a thoroughgoing personal relationship between pastor and client. I hope to show at a later point that there is no necessary incompatibility, that the functional role is only a mode of expressing something deeper which is aiming at the realization of personality. But the conflict does exist where emphasis is laid on the official position of the minister and it leads some, as we have seen, to argue that the parish priest cannot be a true counsellor. Partly this is because he cannot be divested in the eyes of his client from his authoritative role and partly because he himself does not believe he ought entirely to relinquish his authority even in the counselling situation. If he tries to make the switch from one role to another which he feels is incompatible with it, it is almost impossible for him to be sincere and he is bound to fail. Such a minister ought not to attempt counselling. He can give pastoral care which may be very fruitful, but it will be of the paternal type.

UNCONSCIOUS MOTIVES

Those who undertake pastoral care of the counselling kind ought to bear in mind that they are certain to have unconscious motives of their own which will enter into the counselling relationship, so they should be constantly on the alert to detect them. These motives are active in influencing the choice of the ministry as a career. I say "influencing" rather than "determining", for alongside the unconscious motives there are always conscious ones and the two sets work together in the choice, although the ends and satisfactions they strive for may be divergent and even opposed.

I do not intend to elaborate on the conscious reasons for becoming a candidate for ordination to the ministry. They are well known and in themselves are honest and reasonable. The office gives an opportunity to serve God and man, it leads to interesting work and is in the highest degree conformable to the personal dignity of a human being. The fact that I do not say more about these reasons does not mean that I undervalue them or question their validity. It is simply that they are easily recognized, whereas the unconscious motives working in him are unknown, and may even be unsuspected, by the candidate. The ministry has special attractions for men with strong repressions. A survey carried out some years ago in the United States led to the conclusion that among candidates for ordination there is a large proportion of "passive dependents", that is, men unconsciously seeking to safeguard their infantile attitudes. They are not aiming to give but to get something, largely safety from the challenge to grow up. The Church will have for the most to carry them.

We should not be surprised that this should be the case. Unconscious motives are bound to operate in the choice of any profession and an investigation might show analogous figures for the professions comparable to the ministry, simply because a large part of the community is made up of "passive dependents". We should, however, anticipate that the ministry will draw them for the reason that God and the Church are intimately related to infantile images of father and mother, and thinking about them grows out of these images, and the association of ideas, and sentiments, is deliberately fostered by much teaching in the Church. Yet most of our deepest repressions originate from conflicting images and desires of an infantile character concerned with the parents, so it is almost inevitable that they should manifest themselves in the field of religion in obedience to "God the Father", and in the service of "Mother Church".

Ministers and candidates for the ministry often question the soundness of their own motives, with the result that they are led into bewilderment and indecision. The questioning is apt to be on the conscious level, weighing validity of reasons, whereas everyone should suspect the probability that unconscious motives are at work, and should endeavour to bring them into the open. Some of the satisfactions which make the ministry attractive to men suffering from some inner conflict or uncertainty are fairly obvious, although of course, a given individual may not be aware that they are active in him, since his need is unconscious. It is advisable for a pastor to watch his own reactions to detect any signs betraying their presence in him.

Among the commonest of the attractions we can set the following. First the office is one of high social status. It certainly has been in the past and although there may be some diminution in modern society respect is paid to the clergy. To be an ordained minister is to have social significance, one of the deepest needs of the human spirit and one which is often frustrated in infancy and childhood, where "children should be seen and not heard"; or, more serious, they get the feeling of not being loved, and need in later life to get the assurance of respect from the position they hold, since they do not feel able to claim it for themselves as persons. The office, too, confers authority and gives its holder the right to "lay down the law". He may have suffered in his early years from others wielding authority over him when he was helpless to reply and now he can revel in the authority conferred on him. He does it in the name of God and feels very virtuous in doing so, and no one can reply to him. He is aggrandized by the feeling of power that comes from the exercise of this authority in teaching and also from the fact that in various ways he has power over people's lives, since he is given charge over them. His tenure of office is secure, particularly in the Anglican Church, and security is a basic need. And with security goes freedom; there is surprisingly little oversight of his work and he is free to carry it on as seems best to him. He is his own boss and sets his own times, works at whatever pace he likes, does as much or as little as he pleases.

It is to be expected that any or all these may be present in some degree as motives influencing the choice of the ministry as a career. There is no reason why they should not, for they belong to the office. What matters is the extent to which they operate, for if they are strong they can distort the conscious reasons for the choice and make them merely rationalizations for a decision based on the unconscious motives. This latter is most likely to occur in men who are the victims of deeper repressions seeking satisfactions which must be disguised because the repressed form is forbidden. When we look at some of the repressions which commonly occur we see how they can get satisfaction in ministerial work. Deep unconscious feelings of guilt are almost universal. These can be eased by accepting hardship and suffering, and the ministry is often presented as a "sacrifice", by which is meant giving up of pleasures and benefits which are considered desirable. Certainly the material rewards are few, not comparable with other professions, but the proper justification for choosing it as a career is that it is more satisfying to the whole man at the highest level of his development than any other. It is only sacrifice in the sense of dedication. What is given up is more than compensated for by the personal fulfilment it brings. "Who for the joy that was set before him endured the cross, despising the shame. . . ." We cannot buy our way out of guilt; it can only be undone by forgiveness.

The minister has to do a lot of talking. In some instances it is the chief exercise of his calling: preaching, teaching, advising, exhorting. It offers great opportunities for the satisfaction of oral fixations. These are very common. They can combine with others to find their expression in ministerial utterance. It is all too common to find clergy who cannot keep silent or who get what is almost a sensual enjoyment from "proclaiming the word". Or it may be a hidden "exhibitionism" which is at work, leading perhaps to shyness in personal demeanour, but getting satisfaction in donning richly coloured vestments and parading ceremonially in them, or in being the centre of attention when one is in the high pulpit. In either case the self-display is part of one's duty and therefore allowed. One of the commonest repressions is of aggressive impulses and these can find their outlet in fierce condemnation of sin and sinners, in attacks upon the "declining morals of the present generation", or the "materialism" of the age, or upon "warmongers" and so on and so on. Denunciations from the pulpit seem to give much satisfaction and a sense of fulfilment to the preacher and to the congregation as well, who, troubled by the same repressions, get a vicarious satisfaction by identifying themselves with the preacher. In a gentler way we have those clergy who long to rescue people from sin or suffering or oppression, an aspiration which originates in some cases from fixation in the infantile desire to rescue the beloved and beautiful mother from the father. The strength and extent of this fixation is evidenced by the number of beautiful damsels who have to be rescued by gallant knights from dragons or other ogres in fairy tales or from villains or cruel fathers or stepfathers in romances. Into the same group of hidden fixations we can put those who seek ordination because in doing so they are submitting to the primal father of their infancy and have not come to terms with the real father as they grew up.

These are only a few brief illustrations of the unconscious motives which the pastor may carry with him into his work. Before we go on to examine what should be done about them, let us look at what happens in the candidate's training and in his early years of work as a minister.

TRAINING

In college or university he is expected to spend up to three or four years on many branches of theology, mainly occupied in the academic or theoretical study of the Bible, doctrine, Church history, ethics, liturgy. Very little time is given to psychology, anthropology, sociology, science, economics, politics—that is, to the study of man as he is in the world. The emphasis is much more on ideas than on people and his values are shaped accordingly. He gets some practical training but the amount varies from place to place and denomination to denomination. It usually emphasizes method and organization—how to run Sunday schools, youth clubs, parish visiting. I was told some years ago by a minister who worked in the Sunday school of the First Baptist Church in Dallas, Texas (one of the outstanding examples of efficiency in the United States), that while he was there business men were sending their young executives there to learn business organization and methods. Organizational efficiency is apt to be highly regarded by Church authorities. Even where psychological training is given it is apt to emphasize technique—in preaching, for instance—as this book may appear to be doing: how we can "put across" our message to people, how we can influence them.

In other words the candidate is given a professional training and he emerges with the impression that he is an expert or on the way to becoming one. But an expert in what? In theology perhaps; in ideas about religion. Because he has been trained, accepted, and ordained by the responsible authorities he almost inevitably sees himself occupying a position of authority and is encouraged to behave as one. The temptation all too frequently is to assume implicitly that it also means superiority, with the responsibility of raising his flock up to his level of enlightenment and virtue. It may be thought that this is a caricature of what really happens and that I have omitted reference to compensating features in the training, such as the practice of prayer, the emphasis on humility (too often appearing as false modesty), and the whole effort to create selflessness in the minister to be. I willingly concede that I have drawn a one-sided picture, because I am concerned to point to weaknesses that may be present, but it has to be admitted that it is part of the total picture and that the results of the training are frequently as I have described them. Some years ago a young man working in a factory in the North of England decided to seek ordination. He was so beloved by his workmates in the factory that they subscribed the funds needed to give him his training in a theological college. After two years he came back to visit the factory and those who met him came in horror to the Church authorities to demand "What have you done to our Bill?"

POST-ORDINATION EXPERIENCE

Let us follow our somewhat weaker brother into his parish after he has been ordained. In some Churches he is now entitled to be called "Father" and he tries to live up to the role. Usually it is in a benevolent manner, loving and caring for his children, but not far below the kindly surface is the judgmental attitude ready to rebuke and chastise the erring. The members of his flock and others who come to him for advice and help approach him in the same spirit. They pay him courtesy and respect and sometimes even more, for he is now "reverend", to be revered. It is true that the reverence is paid to the representative of God, not to the person, but it is difficult for him to separate the two roles in himself.

Some ministers find this very satisfying and they do not want to change it. They place importance on the representative character of their office and gladly accept the reverence accorded to them as right and proper. Others challenge it as a one-way channelling of communication preventing the basic mutual communication which is only possible in a true personal relationship. For while the minister is a representative he is also a person, subject to the imperfections of men, and if emphasis is laid on the office to the exclusion of the men it depersonalizes the office, making it entirely functional, and at the same time allows the failures of the man to demean the office in some measure at least. The danger is that the unconscious biases—towards power, towards authority—will colour his interpretation of his office and may lead him to seek emotional satisfactions in it which belong to the office and not to himself. This may bring about a dictatorial trend rendering good pastoral work impossible.

Another line of development, a very common one, is when work in the parish leads him to feel a sense of inadequacy in face of the opportunities and responsibilities of his office. The view in advance of the ministry is inevitably foreshortened and in some measure romantic. We see the value, the truth, and the excitement of religion, and we feel that it should be easy to win people to our way of thinking. But the job does not turn out like that. People are not sinners ripe for conversion or even very interested in the theology with which we have been filled. They are ordinary human beings, sinners no doubt, but wrapped up in their own concerns. They are very polite to the minister and tell him how much they enjoyed his sermon or his visit or the "beautiful service", but somehow it does not seem to have any marked effect on their lives. What he talks about is either trivial or irrelevant, a kind of Church jargon which does not seem to have any real importance in the day-to-day struggle to cope with the world and live with other people. So he gets discouraged, seeing no positive return for his earnest labours.

Yet a ray of hope appears. People have their problems, big problems sometimes, and they start bringing them to him. He wants to help them but it is harder than he had supposed. Telling them about God's love and forgiveness, explaining how they ought to live, saying prayers for them and with them does not dissolve away the problems even when it gives them some comfort. From what he was taught the problems ought to disappear instead of appearing intractable. So the minister feels inadequate. He wishes he had had a better training in pastoral psychology, for he thinks that lack of that may be the cause of his failure. But he is looking at it in the nature of a "gimmick", a magical technique to replace the magical formula of prayer or exhortation which failed to work.

So the office he sought for excellent reasons turns out to be empty, or he himself feels empty and loses heart. It is too late to do anything else, and besides he feels he would "let the side down" if he gave up the ministry. It would also be a confession of failure, and being, as I postulated, one of the weaker brethren, he cannot face that openly. What does he do? There are many different ways of reacting. Some familiar ones are worth looking at:

1. He may regress into what is in effect a fantasy world, a world of emphasis on magical incantations, shutting himself, his message, and, so far as he can achieve it, his congregation off from the concerns of everyday life. The most important thing and the test of "goodness" is to attend church services. "Spirit" is exalted at the cost of matter, "holiness" counts above everything, prayer is no longer the accompaniment or interpretation of work, it is all that is needed. God is the great magician.

2. He may get his satisfactions by giving free play to his aggression. He attacks those who stay away from Church. The morals of the present generation are corrupted, materialism is rampant on every side, the values of the community

are degenerating, divorce, delinquency, crime on the increase. It is the world that has failed, not he.

3. Sometimes, perhaps most often, he just drifts on, un-
happy, frustrated, disappointed, having lost inspiration and
hope, withdrawing more and more within himself, not knowing what to say to people, over-valuing what little successes
come his way.

4. He may take to gimmicks, seeking a magic spell to achieve
success, like taking a service for athletes in a track suit or
starting one for firemen with an alarm bell. He takes up
new movements—the Liturgical Movement, Parish and
People's Movement, Youth Clubs, C.N.D.—not because these
are good in themselves but to him they are gimmicks that
he may use to get people to church or to give him the feeling
of significance which he desperately needs. Many years ago
a prominent minister with an important and popular church
asked a colleague of mine, "What is this Lent business? Is it
something I could use?" Among the gimmicks much sought
after nowadays is pastoral counselling. It is treated as a
technique of dealing with people and it becomes a substitute
for religious concern instead of an expression of it. The
sketchy training he has had in college and the book or two
he has read since the end of his course are not adequate to
fit him for the work; he is not able to cope there in spite of
the sense of power which he gets from trying to be a counsellor.

5. A happier alternative is that he should wake up to the
fact that his student conception of the ministry was a romantic one and did not take account of the real values to be
found in it. He has met people and come to the understanding that they are the important thing and that the office of
the pastor gives him the opportunity of meeting people at
the deepest level of their being and that living with them at
that level is the essence of his vocation rather than holding
a superior position from which to ladle out spiritual food.

He struggles to learn how to communicate with them, to share himself with them and share in them, and in so doing learns in part to understand himself and see something of his own weaknesses. Instead of running away from his failures he uses them to find out what he is really like, and this helps him to be a real person instead of a symbol or mouthpiece to those he meets. His weaknesses no longer become a hindrance in his work; they may even be an asset, for they make him more "human", more identifiable as a person, to his parishioners. For this he must recognize them himself and accept them as part of him. It is weakness unrecognized and unacknowledged by oneself that is a hindrance, weakness that is not deliberately offered to God as part of self-dedication. Two clergy of my acquaintance are exhibitionists. One knows he is and openly acknowledges it; the other does not, or, if he does, tries to hide it even from himself. The former is highly successful in his work and can use his exhibitionism in a fruitful way. The second, despite great gifts, is a failure, for he gets between people and God, by focusing attention on himself.

What safeguards can be set up to protect men from entering the ministry from false motives and the Church from the failures which will follow?—and how can clergy with such weaknesses be helped both in their work and in themselves? A number of lines of action suggest themselves.

1. The American Episcopal Church (Anglican) requires a psychiatric examination of every candidate before he is accepted for training. It is admitted that this is often cursory but many psychiatrists appointed for this take it seriously. This screening is not for the rejection of candidates on psychological grounds, although as might be expected some bishops tend to use it this way and try to make the psychiatrist responsible for turning men down. The intention and the great value of the psychiatric examination is that if it

is carried out thoroughly it usually reveals the hidden weakness in the candidate. It then becomes possible to take appropriate steps to deal with the weakness. As I said just now, a weakness discovered and accepted in and by the candidate may become a source of strength, if it is used in the right way. Homosexuality, with its great potential for friendship on the spiritual level, can be such a motive.

2. Measures to deal with discovered weaknesses can be taken in the college where the candidate is trained, or elsewhere as part of his training. He can be given the individual tutorial and counselling help, even, if need be, psychotherapy, which will correct his weakness, and there should be specialists on the staff full or part time to do this work.

3. All candidates should be given thorough training in pastoral care/counselling, even at the cost of reducing the load of academic theological training which they at present have to carry. It should include both training in the theory of personality development and group dynamics and practical training in the dynamics of personal relationships.

4. Provision should be made for post-ordination "in-service" training. Before they are ordained ministers are not directly aware of the problems and difficulties which come to them in the exercise of their office. They do not know what questions to ask or what their own emotional reactions will be. After, say, five years in office they will know where they most need help and guidance both for themselves and for the clients who have come to them for help.

5. Provision should be made where possible—though this may often be a matter for local or individual initiative—for continuous training in the forms suggested in an earlier chapter. These involve referral of clients to a pastoral counselling clinic and co-operation with it; consultation over cases with a psychotherapist; groups of clergy meeting together under the guidance of a psychotherapist, or some

similar scheme which local conditions make it possible to arrange. Further, there is need of more courses to be set up at training centres which may be taken by clergy on a part-time basis. Such courses are now provided at the Tavistock Clinic, London, at the University of Birmingham, and at the Clinical Theology Association, Nottingham, and others are being organized. These courses, however, need to take into account the distinction I have been at pains to emphasize between general pastoral care/counselling and specialist counselling.

Developments are taking place so rapidly that there is good reason to hope that before long some training may be available for all ordinands and clergy. The realization of the value of it is constantly growing, but the sheer difficulty of finding the means, in personnel, in money, and in time, to provide the training and take full advantage of it when it is available is a serious obstacle in the way of quick progress. One of the greatest needs is to provide an adequate theological reconciliation between the traditional religious doctrine of man, and of God, too, and the knowledge which comes from modern psychology. Other disciplines have their contribution to make but they lie outside the scope of this book. Consideration of the lines this reconciliation may take must be reserved for the final chapter.

8

Wrongdoing, Sin, and Moral Disease

The matters we have been considering in the last few chapters come to a head in what is the central problem for the pastor. It is a problem of great theoretical and practical significance, but like all human problems it has many facets and therefore it is difficult to define. On the practical side it appears as a dilemma for the pastor: experience shows that successful counselling requires him to accept the client as he is, to refrain from criticizing or condemning him for his actions, yet the pastor is trained to uphold the standards of conduct which have been broken by the client. The client certainly was the doer of the acts, so he is in that sense responsible for them. The acts cannot be separated from the agent, they are part of him, the expression of what he is. To condemn them is to condemn what he is. It is far too facile to say, "Forgive the sinner and condemn the sin". The sin must be accepted and loved with the sinner. This is the practical dilemma for the pastor. Acceptance does not mean blindness, an inability or refusal to see the quality of the act committed, any more than love for the sinner implies failure to see the state of his character. "While we were yet sinners Christ died for us" (Rom. 5. 8) carries with it the overtone that God loves us as sinners and acted to redeem us *because* we were sinners. We must be careful not to carry this reasoning too far. All we can say is that God loves sinners and saints alike. The pastor is expected to have the same godly attitude, but how can he avoid condemning his client when he knows that he does things which in the pastor's judgment are evil things? This is tantamount to asking how can he become godlike. If the client is regarded as a sick man and not a wrongdoer the dilemma disappears. Hence the importance of the theoretical question whether men are sinful or are sick, deliberate and wilful doers of what they know to be evil or victims of compulsions which take away their freedom. The pastor must come to terms with this question if he is to learn how to withhold condemnation of his client. It is far more complex than is commonly assumed, so we must examine it more closely.

The common assumption is that it is easy to commit what we call sin or wrongdoing. It must be, because it is so universal. Yet the moment we look at the psychological forces involved we are compelled to believe that it must on the contrary require considerable effort to do wrong, if wrong consists in overcoming the urges on the side of right. Arrayed against it is, first, the fear of punishment to deter us. Considerations of prudence must make us hesitate about doing anything which will involve sanctions. The punishment may be imminent in parental wrath, delayed in matters of lawbreaking by the need to go through the legal processes of arrest and trial, or be anticipated only after death as divine judgment, except in those people who see God's action as immediate. Many people advocate severity of punishment of all these kinds as, they believe, an effective deterrent against wrongdoing. Then there is the social sanction, the fear of loss of approval, or active disapproval, from those whose regard is valued. This is a powerful force. The need to be approved, loved, by his parents is very strong in the young child, one of the most potent factors not only in influencing his behaviour but in shaping the structure of his personality. The need extends to a wider circle as the individual grows, and in religious people is referred to God, when it may be a stronger sanction than any fear of punishment in hell. Simply to be condemned by God is to many people the ultimate punishment, far more effective as a sanction than the pains that the demons in hell might inflict. The symbol of the watching eye indicates that we cannot escape observation by God and avoid his disapproval of our wrongdoing. Thirdly, we are governed by our conscience, which we recognize as imposing unconditional obligation upon us and which categorically forbids wrongdoing. This is the super-ego in us, which by its nature is our inner authority regulating our conduct, and it can only be overcome by superior psychological force. Fourthly, we are also in part governed by our ego-ideal, our ideal of our true selves, containing in it our self-respect, which urges us at all times to goodness. We might add to these love of our fellow men as probably in the end the strongest of all motives when it is attained, but it is not easy to isolate it as a separate motive, nor is it so universally present as the four I have mentioned.

These are all strong forces, varying of course with different individuals, yet in the face of them men do things they believe to be wrong. Theologians ascribe this to "original sin", some kind of in-built tendency to do wrong, and non-religious people explain it in various ways that are "natural" to man—the vestigial effects of evolution, the unreasonableness of the demands of the moral code, and so on. All that either party succeeds in doing is to emphasize the fact that wrongdoing does occur. We must search more deeply to discover why.

Before going on to discuss what may be done to help alleviate the burden of guilt I should clear away the confusion which may result from my use of "sin" and "wrongdoing" as equivalent terms. The word "sin" has a theological reference. Those who believe in God experience their wrongdoing as offences against God, transgressions of his will. Those who have no belief in God, or only a vague belief in some impersonal power, think of their wrongdoing as a betrayal of themselves, a failure in their integrity because they have departed from the standard of good conduct which they have accepted. Theirs is a moral judgment, not a theological one. Behind the theological lies also a moral judgment, but the moral standard is centred in God. Because persisting unconscious parent images are also attached to God, attitudes derived from them, such as infantile guilt and fear, may enter into moral guilt to intensify them. Neurotic guilt over having committed "the inforgivable sin" is a case in point. However, as we shall see, whether the client declares himself to be guilty of sin or moral wrongdoing, the source of the guilty feeling is the attack by the super-ego on the ego, an inner tension.

The word "sin" is used to denote two kinds of action. The first, which theologians call "actual sin", is to do something which we believe to be wrong. The second, called "formal sin", is to do something which we do not believe to be wrong (we may even believe that it is right), but which in fact is wrong. Let us put aside here the very difficult question of how an act may be objectively determined to be wrong, since we are concerned with questions of motive.

ACTUAL SIN

Actual sin implies that the sinner had knowledge of what he is doing, he believes it to be wrong, and he freely chooses to do it. It is not enough for him merely to know that other people believe it to be wrong. That would simply be a social standard. The moral standard by which actual sin is measured must be an inner one, the rule of conscience. The rule which is broken by the individual must be accepted by him with that sense of unconditional obligation which characterizes moral principles. This means that it must be embodied in the individual's super-ego and invested with the authority which the latter exercises over the ego and be assented to by the ego.

We can now analyse more precisely what happens in the mind when a wrong action is committed. The pressure to do it comes from the id, which is the primary source of desire. The psychic energies exercised by the ego and super-ego are derived by these structures from the id in the course of growth, but throughout life the id continues its primary function of initiating desire. Once a desire is formed it moves towards the ego to get expression. Before the desire reaches consciousness it is surveyed by those parts of the ego and super-ego which reach into the unconscious. It may be opposed at this level and repressed so that it does not reach consciousness, and the question of actual sin does not arise. If the desire is allowed into consciousness there are three alternatives open to the ego.

1. The ego can resist it under the domination of the massive forces mentioned earlier which oppose doing anything believed to be wrong. Once an impulse has become conscious it is examined by the conscience aspect of the super-ego and if it is judged to be wrong the super-ego asserts its authority over the ego and forbids the action. The result is a locking of the forces, and the energies of the total self are used up in the battle. In most cases some degree of repression follows, leading in turn to unrecognized substitute forms of expression.

2. A satisfactory compromise action is found. Instead, for instance, of attacking someone who has aroused our anger we go and chop up wood and satisfy our destructive impulses in that way.

3. The ego can give way and the sinful act is performed. It is with this alternative that we are at present concerned.

The consequence of doing what we believe to be wrong is a feeling of guilt. The guilt is usually coloured by other feelings, a sense of unworthiness, of uncleanness, of being under condemnation, of having cut oneself off from one's fellows, of remorse, and a wish to undo the act. The core of the feeling of guilt is the condemnation by the super-ego. It attacks the ego and requires it to re-assert the validity of the broken law. This re-assertion is made when the ego submits with contrition and acceptance of blame, acknowledging that what has been done is wrong.

In accepting blame the ego is implicitly claiming freedom of choice and responsibility for the action. "I could have resisted the impulse." Sometimes there is added "if I had wanted to". That the lack of a desire to resist completely is not a failure of the ego but indicates a deeper fault is always overlooked, and the ego accepts the blame for not wanting to resist. It should be said at once that it is the nature of the ego, as the integrative function of the mind, to claim full responsibility, and therefore freedom, over as much of mental life as becomes conscious. The feeling of freedom is the ego in action; without it there can be no ego. Hence guilt is an inevitable reaction of wrongdoing.

This feeling of freedom, however subjectively convincing, may be an illusion, though a necessary device to safeguard the ego. The wrong act may be the result of psychological forces over which the ego has no control and therefore there is no choice possible. It may be that unconscious motives are operating and that the ego has to invent rationalizations to explain, excuse, or simply to describe what has happened, because without the rationalization the sense of freedom would be destroyed.

Let us use the term moral disease to describe behaviour which would be called wrongdoing if done from free choice but in which the freedom of the ego is impaired, even though the subject is not aware of it but believes he was acting freely. Some instances of wrongdoing are clearly recognized as moral disease. An insane person is not held responsible for his actions, however bad they may be. In law such a person is held "not fit to plead". There is coming to be recognized a class of persons who, while not classified as insane, have a diminished sense of responsibility. It is very difficult to define this state but its characteristic is the temporary or permanent inability to invoke the forces I have mentioned which restrain impulses believed to be wrong. A further class is made up of those people who suffer from compulsions of various kinds. Compulsive actions, e.g. handwashing, may be of a morally innocent character, but frequently they are rated as immoral. Common examples of this are stealing by kleptomaniacs, indecent exposure, and probably cases of assault and murder of little children. In these the unconscious impulse has been out of the control of the ego, just because it is unconscious.

In less severe cases, where the neurosis or psychosis is not obvious, unconscious factors can still operate, for instance in such things as bad temper, greediness, covetousness, compulsive masturbation. The ego may claim full responsibility, accept blame and feel guilty, but there can be also a recognition of helplessness even when the act is admitted. "The evil which I would not that I practise . . . But if what I would not, that I do, it is no more I that do it, but sin which dwelleth in me. . . . O wretched man than I am!" (Rom. 7. 19–20, 24).

Frequently we meet people who are suffering from a sense of guilt for which there is no obvious justification. The guilt may be free floating, a sense of unworthiness, not attached to any particular acts, or it may be attached to minor peccadilloes, exaggerating their gravity out of all proportion, as frequently happens in periods of mourning, or in that common character trait of scrupulosity against which Baron von Hügel warned in his *Letters to a Niece,* cautioning her not to indulge in a "spiritual flea-hunt". In such cases the validity of the alleged reason for guilt may be doubted, but the reality of the feeling should not be questioned. It is due to the attack by the super-ego on wishes which remain unconscious. These have "psychological reality"; they are treated as actual deeds, since neither the id nor the super-ego, but only the ego, distinguishes between fantasy and reality. The wishes remain unconscious but the feeling of guilt penetrates into consciousness. It may not always do so It also may remain unconscious, actively influencing behaviour. In that case psychotherapy is needed to deal with it.

In all these cases the pressure of unconscious motives

influencing conduct limits the freedom of the ego and the wrongdoing is not done of free choice, so actual sin is not involved. The feeling of freedom, where it occurs, and the sense of guilt reflect the inter-relations of the different functions or structures of the total mind. Where the ego is really free to choose it is able to summon to its aid the forces which oppose wrongdoing and by those means control conduct. It is certain that the clients who seek aid of the pastor are thus limited in their behaviour and therefore should not be blamed for it, however bad it may seem to be. Once the pastor has grasped this principle his dilemma disappears. He is not condoning sin by accepting and loving the sinner. The sinner has not chosen sin, it is the outcome of faults in his growth. This is true even of seemingly normal healthy people. Sin is impossible to anyone who is completely free. "If thine eye be single, thy whole body shall be full of light" (Matt. 6. 22).

FORMAL SIN

The question of formal sin is a different matter. The sinner is not to be blamed for his sin but the character of his act should be recognized. Though his ego or conscious self was under constraint his total self was responsible for what he did and he cannot repudiate it. To say that it was caused by "the sin which dwelleth in me" is not an explanation but a description of the state of the personality and is a plea for help.

St Paul was here on the borderline between actual and formal sin. He recognized the "sinful" character of his acts but knew that he was not free to stop them. In formal sin the acts are committed in the belief that they are right, or at least innocent, not wrong. The regular example of this is the torturers of the Inquisition who firmly believed they were doing God's will in trying to compel "heretics" to accept the "true faith". While most people would now agree that they were doing evil, there is still the difficulty of establishing a standard which proves that an act is wrong in some absolute sense, such as the will of God. That lies completely beyond the scope of this book, but for practical purposes we may assume that there is some such standard although no one can be certain that he knows what it is. Some of course believe that they do, and most men, while not going to this extreme of conviction, judge acts as good or bad in themselves, irrespective of the conscience of the doer. But it is worth noting that if God judges some act as bad in itself —going to war, let us say—God also requires a man to do what he believes to be right (if we regard conscience as man's highest sanction of conduct); and so we are brought to the difficult conclusion that God asks men to do what is bad as an act of goodness. The difficulties which this proposition raises is enough in itself to make us hesitate, certainly as pastors, about making moral judgments on the acts of clients.

The matter needs to be seen in a wider perspective. Instead of trying to judge each act by some postulated and at best partially understood absolute criterion of goodness, we should assess human conduct in terms of the development of personality. Acts cannot be judged in isolation. Greed and sensuality in a baby are both permissible and good, but as he grows they should be sublimated into other modes of behaviour. We have already seen that what we call actual sin is the result of defective development. The same holds for formal sin. It is usually the result of persisting infantile or childish attitudes and values, not merely in the moral standards accepted but in failure to develop to maturity in emotional integration and in reasoned adjustment to the real world of persons and things. When we become men we should "put away childish things", but it is our misfortune, not our fault, if we fail to become fully men.

There is one feature of moral growth which illustrates this clearly. While we think we are doing right, our conscience does not trouble us, we have no sense of guilt. If, however, our moral sense for some reason grows—and there

are many factors which should lead us to expect this to happen—we may look back on actions we did believing them
to be right and we now condemn them as wrong. This is
what we may call "deferred guilt". When Isaiah saw the
vision of God in the Temple his conscience was quickened
and it wrung the cry from him "Woe is me! for I am undone;
because I am a man of unclean lips, and I dwell in the midst
of a people of unclean lips!" (Isa. 6. 5).

There is one special form of this deferred guilt feeling
which is not only part of growing up but is an essential con-
stituent of developed human nature. We saw (Chapter 5)
that the child emerges from the conflicts of later infancy
by introjecting the images he has formed of his parents,
thereby setting up his super-ego as a permanent part of the
structure of his mind. This enables him to control, by conscious suppression or unconscious repression, those desires
which were contrary to the wishes and authority of the
parents and therefore (psychologically) dangerous. The fears
of the child had psychological reality and were not the result
of threats or punishment by the parents, though these can
intensify them. Once the super-ego is formed it looks back
on past acts as well as on the continuing desires with a *moral*
judgment, and a sense of guilt inevitably develops. But the
desires which compelled the formation of the super-ego
were at the beginning only a danger situation, not a moral
one. They were not judged as wrong, only as dangerous.
Without the Oedipal conflicts no super-ego and therefore
no conscience proper would be formed, hence we all must
carry with us this sense of having done wrong. We may call
this "original guilt". Since it comes out of the resolution of
the Oedipus Complex it is directed most strongly towards
incest and parricide, which Freud called the "primal sins".
An over-strong super-ego is prone to concentrate its attacks,
openly or in the unconscious, on sex and rebellion, impurity
and defiance of authority. One might add, particularly when
they are manifested in adolescents, for adolescence is the
period of final escape from the family.

ORIGINAL SIN

There is still another source of guilt feelings, one which perhaps is the most significant of all. It is the one which lies behind the theological doctrine of Original Sin. We cannot here go into the theological aspects of it nor launch upon an analysis of why the explanations of it as due to an historical fall or a quasi-historical "pre-cosmic" fall are unsatisfactory. We are concerned to understand the psychological forces involved in the behaviour which has made it necessary to formulate some doctrine of original sin. There is need for an explanation, since the doing of sinful acts is a hard fact despite the forces opposing this. We have seen that this can be explained by inadequate integration of the personality. Similarly the contagiousness of sin may be due to the same cause. But this misses the point of the doctrine of original sin, for this is aimed to explain what seems to be an unquestionable feature of human conduct—that we are disposed to sin, always ready to yield to temptation, that it is our nature to do so whether or not we are fully integrated. This element of our nature is not to be confused with the "actual sins" we may commit; it is that in us which must make us feel unworthy, however "good" we are, that which Jesus meant when he said "when ye shall have done all the things that are commanded you, say, We are unprofitable servants" (Luke 17. 10).

The explanation is relatively simple. We form as part of our total self an ego-ideal which we identify as our true self. It is what we want to be and what we think we ought to be. It is the dynamic positive source of our constant striving to be better than we are. It is built up from many elements: from the desire to be loved by our parents and to be what we imagine they want us to be; from the desire to be like them as in infancy (and perhaps later) we see them; from our admiration of other people whom we come to know or know about and our desire to please them; from our identification with them; from our reflections about our experience, and so on. Because it is an ideal self we thus construct it is always ahead of what we know our actual ego to be. We must by its very nature fall short of the ideal. The result of believing that we have attained to the ideal is mania—uncontrollable madness. Thus unless we are mad there is always a gap between what we are and what we see we ought to be and this gap is an essential part of our nature. However hard we try we cannot close the gap, because the ideal must always move on ahead of us. Since we see the ideal as our true self we must always be aware of "missing the mark", and feel ourselves as unworthy, as wrongdoers, as "fallen", being below where we ought to be. It is in this sense that "fallenness" is inherent in human nature, but, since it is the result of the effort to be better than we at any time are, Original Sin is not really a fall but a condition of rising. Nevertheless it is a source of guilt feeling which may intensify or be intensified by feelings of guilt coming from other sources.

This very brief analysis of the psychological forces involved in sin and wrongdoing and the consequent feelings of guilt enables us to define the problem they raise for pastoral care and to see the treatment the suffering client needs. As guilt is likely to play some part in every case the handling of it is very important. I said at the beginning of the chapter that there are theoretical and practical aspects. The practical divides into two: how the pastor handles his own reactions, and what help he can give to the client. The first of these also involves the theoretical aspect of morality.

The client comes to the pastor and reveals, either immediately or in later sessions, feelings of guilt over wrongdoing. That he has done wrong may be apparent even if the intensity of the guilt-feeling does not seem appropriate to the gravity of the offence in the eyes of the pastor. The disproportion, either too much or too little, is a warning to the pastor that strong unconscious processes are working and that the wrong act admitted is a screen for something else.

The guilt-feeling is the result of the pressure by the super-ego on the client's ego, but it is his ego which has presented the case to the pastor with the hope of getting help to ease the pressure. The pastor in turn is subject to the working of his own super-ego and if he has not become aware of and accepted the existence of similar impulses in himself his super-ego will drive him to condemn the client for his action. It is not enough to restrain himself from uttering condemnation, though restraint is better than outspoken criticism; for the judgmental attitude will betray itself in other ways, by looks, by hesitations, gestures, tones of voice, and the client will sense it. This condemnation will reinforce the client's own super-ego and intensify the guilt he already feels. His super-ego will be confirmed and his ego weakened. The barrier between them will be transferred to the pastor-client relationship and there will be little hope of the pastor being able to set the client free from his fixations and conflicts. To be a good pastoral counsellor he must have come to terms with himself, that is, got to know his own weaknesses and accepted them, so that there will be no danger of projecting on to his client his condemnation of himself. Instead he will be better able to give understanding and empathy with him and so make available to him the freedom he himself has won.

The pastor gets the ability to come to terms with himself from his practical training in the dynamics of personal relationships and from his actual experience as a pastor. The training is based on the same principles as that which is given to psychotherapists and social caseworkers; but there is one important difference in their situations which may affect the approach to him, the demands made upon him, and his own conception of what he must try to give to his client. Psychotherapist, caseworker, and pastor all put their counselling skills and experience to the service of their clients, but the pastor in addition holds a philosophy of life which he feels impelled to impart, for it is that which gives final meaning to his office. He believes himself called by God (in whatever sense he interprets this) to be a minister and cannot ignore the responsibility to speak on behalf of God. Nor can he overlook his duty to represent the Church to which he belongs, whose beliefs, traditions, and values he has accepted in his own way. It may well be that he conceives it his supreme duty to proclaim his message about God and/or to uphold as absolute the duty of all to keep unbroken what is accepted generally as the moral law. In either case he cannot be client-centred, non-directive in his pastoral counselling. He must, to be true to himself and so to his client, be directive, aiming to bring the latter to the right view of life or the right way of living. And this must be his aim, even if it allows for freedom for the client to differ in some measure from his views and values. On the other hand, he may interpret his whole vocation as being throughout people-centred. His religion is expressed in his living with people and his teaching of faith and morals is secondary, designed to help people to be themselves.

This is the theoretical problem to which I have referred. The pastor cannot get the answer to it from his practical training, though he may get some evidence to influence his thinking. He has to decide on wider grounds what vocation to the ministry means, and choose between the broad alternatives of seeing himself called to live a life among his people through which they may come to know God for themselves, or on the other hand as called primarily to proclaim and defend truth and the moral law as he has received them. He needs to bring every aspect of his work under the one point of view or his own integrity will be shattered. I am convinced that the minister is called simply to live a God-filled life with his fellow-men and the belief and morals flow out of that. I shall try to give grounds for this conviction in the last chapter. Meanwhile I would point out that if belief and morals are put first by him the pastor cannot refrain from passing judgment on his client and that militates against successful pastoral counselling. With that attitude he should use other methods of discharging his pastoral duties. He is more concerned to produce right behaviour from his client than right growth, to deal with what are really the symptoms and not the disease itself. He does not in fact see his client as sick but as weak, erring, ignorant. He may deal with him sternly or with loving tenderness, but his endeavour will be to give supportive treatment by persuasion, exhortation, sympathy, or any other moral pressure he can bring to bear. He knows clearly the result he wants to produce.

The other kind of pastor who is truly a counsellor does not know, except in abstract terms, what will result from his work. He is aware that his client is in bondage, unable to make a free choice because of his impaired development. He wants to set him free, to help him grow into a unity, but he cannot tell in advance what in a given case the particular result will be. He has to have faith in his client and in the processes of growth. This faces him with the second practical problem to which I have referred. The first was how to integrate himself, the second is what is the help he can give to the client that he in turn can find freedom and unitary selfhood. That must be the subject of the next chapter.

9

Confession, Counselling, and Forgiveness

So far as is possible in the simplified and short exposition this book allows we have now generalized the problem of counselling in so far as it forms part of the varied work the parish priest has to do. The specialist pastoral counsellor, like the psychotherapist, has to take account of special distinctions within the overall problem, such as, for instance, the differences between psychotic and neurotic character types. For the ordinary pastor this is unnecessary, even if it is interesting in itself and useful for his own illumination to have the knowledge. When his client comes to him seeking help he knows that it is a problem of personal development with which he has to deal, that his client has deep inner conflicts resulting from repressions or weak personality formation, that he is suffering from anxiety, dread, fears, doubts, compulsions, self-distrust, ineffectiveness, and that underneath it all—or breaking through in gusts—is buried guilt and anger. The client's ego is too strongly dominated by his super-ego because he has not been able to contain and sublimate the demands of the id and has had to call the super-ego to the assistance of the ego. This has meant mutilation of his self, and he is burdened with guilt. If the root of the trouble lies in the early part of infancy the burden is likely to be of dread and anger, with guilt secondary. The difficulties experienced by the clients will take a great variety of forms. Emotional conflicts are complex and each individual is unique, but it is safe to assume that in spite of the differences, in spite of the fact that sometimes the symptoms are chronic, sometimes occasional, behind them all lies the general pattern of halted development of the personality. Because of inner psychical changes of balance, or of pressures exerted by external circumstances, the ego of the client is no longer able to maintain the degree of control which had hitherto been possible. The pastor's help is needed to re-establish balance.

He has to choose between two general lines of action if he is to give this help. One line is to try to strengthen his client's super-ego so that he can regain control by greater exercise of his "will" and accept renunciations which were beyond his power before the pastor intervened. For instance suppose it is a marital problem, a marriage threatening to break up because of quarrels between the partners. The pastor may talk to them of the sanctity of marriage and of their duties to the children, remind them of the solemn vows they made when they were married, speak of the necessity of sacrifice and so on. He is using the authority attached to him by the client to reinforce the latter's super-ego so that he can fight down the impulses which have been disturbing him. In doing this the pastor is dealing with the symptoms of the disorder in his client's personality, not with the disorder itself. By this means it may be possible to overcome the troublesome symptoms, but it is quite certain that other symptoms will replace them, and the new ones will be of equal emotional force with the old. They may, however, be more socially acceptable or even of (apparently) greater moral worth. A man living a licentious life which troubles him as well as his acquaintances gets "converted" and adopts a rigid puritanical attitude to sex. He has not thereby solved his emotional conflict, for his new attitude may simply be a "reaction formation", forced on him by his need to keep the impulses, which before had got expression, under the control, in the unconscious, of the super-ego.

An allied type of super-ego control is to be seen in cases of dependent personality, where the client may be unable to take decisions and to bear responsibility. He is constantly seeking someone to advise and direct him and he looks for this from the pastor. This is always a great temptation for the pastor. It flatters him and appeals to any longing for authority and power that may be buried in him, giving him a feeling of importance and success. If he undertakes the role he will, however, find himself burdened with having to make decisions for his client, and the latter will tend to evade accepting responsibility for his actions. The pastor has been made the super-ego of his client. Since the pastor is very much less demanding than the client's inner super-ego the result may appear to be a great release of tension in the client, but the latter is confirmed in dependence on him, preventing further growth to maturity.

While in principle neither of these lines—reinforcing the client's super-ego or assuming direction of his life—is correct, it must be admitted that in practice there are occasions when one or other of them has to be adopted, the second of them as a temporary measure to gain time and to build a relationship which then can be used as a means of education in independence, and the first because the pastor simply has not the time available, or the skill required, to give the help that is really needed, and there is no one else at hand to whom he may send his client. These occasions are much rarer than the pastor may suppose and he should always remember that if he feels forced into adopting one of them, or similar measures, he is refusing to give the help which the client's troubles need, and he runs the risk of hardening him in whatever state of disintegration or immaturity he is in.

The second general line of action with any client which the pastor may take is to aim at strengthening the ego and not the super-ego. This is the true method of pastoral counselling. The ego is the organ of integration and the client's need is for integration. He has to be helped to overcome the mal-development which is the root of his trouble; his ego has to be freed from its bondage to his super-ego so that it can handle the demands of the id without being driven into repressing them and use the super-ego as a guide and not an imperious taskmaster. It is the total personality which is involved in the mal-development, id, ego and super-ego, and this means that these three functions have got out of the proper balance of strength, or relationship, which is necessary for healthy growth to maturity. The ego has been weakened in the course of the client's development, for whatever reasons. The outcome will be the symptoms which the client will present as his trouble, but while taking due account of these the pastor must bear in mind that what has to be corrected is the dynamics of the personality. The temporary measures I discussed in the previous section can only deal with the symptoms. It may seem advisable to suppress one symptom in the hope that the one that will take its place may not be so socially disturbing, but suppression of the symptoms does not further mental and spiritual health—even if superficially it appears to do so, for the succeeding one may quite easily take on a religious form. Permanent cure requires a readjustment of the forces at work in the personality.

This brings us to the question of forgiveness. The client needs forgiveness, by himself of himself, and of others against whom he consciously, or more likely unconsciously, holds animosity, forgiveness by the pastor, by his fellows, and by God. In religion we tend to give a theological emphasis to the word, especially where the practice of general and special confession is followed. Speaking psychologically the process is called acceptance. In either case it is recognized to be closely connected with what we mean by love. But there is a basic difference between liturgical or ministerial forgiveness, as practised, and the forgiveness which is involved in pastoral counselling. An examination of this difference is one of the simplest ways of bringing to light the essential nature of counselling.

The use made of confession and absolution differs among the Churches and among the clergy even of one Church, such as the Anglican. Some rely on the individual joining sincerely in a general confession of sin made by or on behalf of the congregation in public worship and/or confession in private prayer to God. Others advocate individual confession of specific acts of sin to a priest in a formal act in which he is the authorized representative of the Church and of God, shown by his wearing the appropriate vestments for the occasion. In the first form assurance of God's forgiveness of sins is given. In the second the priest's function, based on the certainty of God's forgiveness, is to administer that forgiveness. In both cases the forgiveness requires as a condition of its operation the declaration of the sins and true repentance.

It is outside the scope of this book to examine the theological validity of the use of confession in any form, since we are only concerned with its psychological or practical effectiveness on the personality of the penitent, hence I have described the use made of it in the briefest terms possible. But a liturgical act is also a psychological act and it is in that aspect that some further analysis is necessary.

To begin with, the penitent is expected to acknowledge his sins. He must examine himself, his acts and his desires, so that he can declare them. To declare his "sins" he must also see them as transgressions against God or the moral law, the standards he uses by which to judge himself a sinner. This means that he can confess only the sins of which he is conscious, and it means also that he accepts responsibility for what he has done. In discussing the nature of sin in the previous chapter we saw that the ego, which is the seat of consciousness, is compelled by its nature as the integrative function, to accept so far as it is able the responsibility for all the actions of the person, but that this does not mean that in fact it can control them. The sins are the result of unconscious motives which the ego cannot control. The ego cannot confess the true sources of the act, just because they are unconscious. The sinful acts are certainly done by the penitent, but to call them sins is to claim that they were done freely, and this is wrong. The sense of freedom is an illusion in this case, necessary to enable the ego to feel in control of the self, but even so it can give way to the recognition that the sin was caused by unknown forces at work in or on the self, forces vaguely characterised as "human nature", "evil", "the devil" and so on. In his confession the penitent can admit the acts he is aware of doing; he can quite sincerely if mistakenly declare they were done of free choice, or he can claim that something overbore his will; but he cannot confess the unconscious motives which drove him to the acts in question.

The second requirement in a confession is true repentance, contrition for the sins. What repentance is needs clarification, for there is much confusion attached to the term. The Greek word in the New Testament which it translates has the root meaning of "change of mind" or "change of understanding", a new outlook. In current usage repentance conveys more emotional and moral overtones. There is in it sorrow and regret for the action repented, a wish that it had not been done, self-reproach developing into a feeling of guilt, willingness to accept punishment, and some readiness to make amends for harm done. Together with the acknowledgment that it is our act there is repudiation of it as not belonging to the true self, hence it "soils" us, is a "stain" on our character and, like Isaiah in the Temple, we feel "unclean", needing to be "washed" from our sins. We are alienated from God, from our fellows, and from ourselves. We desire restoration of the unity broken by our sin, the sin to be obliterated, and its effects undone. We want to be forgiven. Repentance, in short, as it is commonly understood, is a complex of mixed emotions and judgments in which in any given case one element may dominate. It may be fear, fear of punishment by God, fear of being condemned by one's fellows, of losing their love and respect, fear of the practical consequences which may result from the sin, fear of losing control of oneself in the future. It may be sorrow for the hurt our sin does to other people or shame that we have fallen short of our ideal of ourselves. It may be grief at having offended against God.

One element commonly found in this mixture of emotions

is particularly worth noting because it reveals its source. I am referring to the strong wish that we had not done what we did do. This wish has two aspects to it. First, it involves the tacit acknowledgment that the act was wrong or bad (by whatever standards of conduct we have accepted). That is a normal and healthy element. Secondly, it has in it also a strong wish for the act not to have occurred, that it be obliterated, that we might be as if we had not done it, or that we might be back in the situation before the act so that we could do something better. It scarcely needs to be said that this is impossible, that everyone knows that it is, yet an enormous amount of emotional energy is expended in the unrealistic wish, and this is often taken to be repentance. It is the function of the ego to recognize facts and adjust to them, so when we have this situation it is obvious that the ego of the penitent is being prevented from fully accepting the fact that the sin has been committed or, more precisely, from regulating behaviour in the situation created by the bad act and with regard to the character which it betrays. The act cannot be denied, but the ego refuses to admit that it approved and desired it. It is true that in seeking to receive forgiveness by God the ego is taking steps to deal with the situation but in the case under consideration the forgiveness sought is "wiping clean the slate", annulment of what has been done. In other words, the ego repudiates the motive from the id which has been too strong for it and the super-ego, and the repudiation is the means by which the authority of the super-ego is maintained. What we have is an ego too weak to regulate the demands of the id and a super-ego too dominant to give the ego the freedom it needs for its proper functioning. The strength of the guilt that ensues and the wish for the sin not to have been done is not repentance, it is simply the conflict between the super-ego and the desires of the id.

True repentance is something different. It is an honest facing of the facts, the recognition that not only have we done something bad, but also that we could not have done anything else at the time: that the sin expressed our true nature and we are helpless to do the good we see. We see ourselves revealed in our acts and instead of trying to repudiate them, instead of pouring out our energies in guilt feelings, in remorse, and in vain wishes for what is done not to have been done, we seek the help to change ourselves. It is our character, not our deeds, that is at fault. This means that we need to accept the motives which led to our sins as an essential part of what we are. The ego must acknowledge the id. But this raises a difficulty. The sin was the indication that the ego was too weak to be able to accept and so control the impulses of the id. The ego can only accept those motives of which it is conscious. These it can admit in confession. As we have seen, however, it is the unconscious forces which overcome the forces which fight against sin, so mere confession can never get at the heart of the matter.

What, then, is the value of the practice of confession? We have seen that it can do harm by strengthening the authority of the super-ego at the cost of weakening the ego, or by fixing the penitent in an attitude of dependence on an authority outside himself. But it may do a great deal of good. This in two ways. It can be an educative experience. The necessity for self-examination before confession can focus conscious attention on habits and motives which have been evading scrutiny and so weakening the integration of the personality. And the counsel given by the confessor to the penitent may help the latter to develop his standards (seated in the super-ego) more satisfactorily, not necessarily by making them more stringent. It is often necessary to ease the demands of the super-ego, to inculcate a different conception of goodness. The tendency of penitents is to concentrate on acts rather than attitudes, which may well lead to scrupulosity and the "spiritual flea-hunt" of Baron von Hügel referred to earlier, leaving the major sinfulness unrecognized and unconfessed in favour of minor peccadilloes which are exaggerated. And since it is easier to recognize sins of commission than sins of omission, or to turn omissions into commissions, the negative aspects of morality are usually over-emphasized. Wise counsel can help to correct these tendencies.

The second way in which the practice of confession is beneficial is that the penitent is brought into an environment of love, understanding, and acceptance. This is manifested in the confessor first of all, and his love reflects and conveys the love of God. Thus by the encounter the penitent is given two things he needs: first a human relationship in which he is accepted with love, and second the assurance of God's love, that is, the assurance that the ultimate character of being is not rejection—which as a sinner condemning himself he had feared—and that the harm he has done can be repaired. Because of the love that is shown him by the human confessor and because of the assurance of divine compassion, his guilt, his self-condemnation, is assuaged and hope of new life is restored to him. He is forgiven because he is enabled to forgive himself. He accepts the truth about himself because the environment of love makes it less psychologically threatening and in thus forgiving himself he is enabled to accept God's forgiveness of him. In other words the ego is strengthened and it can more readily support and transform the instinctive demands of the id.

This brief discussion of the psychological working of liturgical confession has had to leave out of account many aspects of it, but it was necessary if we are to see its relation to pastoral counselling. They are not the same thing and they are not optional alternatives as ways of dealing with the same trouble. One difference should be immediately obvious. In confession it is the spiritually and psychologically mature penitent who is most able to gain from it. The disintegrated and mal-developed are more likely to become fixed in their weakness, yet it is these who, judged by their actions, are the greater sinners. They stand in greater need of counselling. It would be going too far to say that saints need confession and sinners counselling, but there is enough truth in it to give point to the saying.

We may list some of the other differences:

The confessor deals with the sins that are conscious and attitudes of which the client may be aware but which he has not brought under the judgment of his moral standards. The counsellor has in mind the unconscious motives of his client and treats the conscious sins as the symptoms, not the real sickness.

The confessor has a moral and religious perspective which he cannot put aside. His penitent has come to him just because he has that perspective, believing that the confessor will understand his self-condemnation (guilt feelings) and mitigate it by taking the burden in some way on himself or on God. The counsellor offers no judgment, no condemnation of his client, but is permissive and accepting. He is more concerned with fact than with moral evaluation, with bringing to the light of recognition the hidden motives of his client.

The confessor is a functionary or agent in virtue of his office as a minister of the Church. He also acts as the agent of God in the same office. He is therefore, particularly in the eyes of the client, both an authoritative and authority figure. He is also an individual person but usually what he is as a person is irrelevant to his declaration of forgiveness to the penitent. We have seen above that his attitude of love, understanding and compassion has a marked healing effect upon the penitent, but even this he exercises as belonging to his office. He strives to be impersonal. The counsellor, on the other hand, acts as a person and enters into a personal, not impersonal, relationship with his client. It is true that he subordinates his own interests to those of the client, around whose inner life the relationship develops, but this is the essential character of the counselling relationship and it corresponds to the needs of the client. It is true also that the client is likely to see the counsellor as an authority figure, a parental substitute, but this is an unconscious attitude, part of his immaturity, which should be dissolved if the counselling develops successfully. I should add here that, while I have described the way confession is generally used, there are movements in all the Churches, both Catholic and Protestant, to make liturgical confession a more personal relationship and to associate it more closely with counselling.

The confessor imposes obligations on his penitent in the form of penance. This has a multiple purpose. It serves as a punishment to mark condemnation of the sins; it sometimes offers a means of reparation for the damage done to others by the sin; it may be in a form calculated to help the penitent strengthen his spiritual life; and above all acceptance of the penance is proof and at the same time confirmation of his penitence, because it aligns him on the side of right against wrong. It thereby strengthens his super-ego. The counsellor, on the other hand, makes no demands, imposes no obligations. While he trusts that his client will recognize the nature of his motives when he comes to know them, he does not want him to repudiate them and try to treat them as alien to what he is. He wants the client to accept the fact that they are part of him. He aims to get the client to work from what he is, rather than from what he believes he ought to be, so there is no question of his asking the client to accept punishment for being what he is.

The confessor usually, though not necessarily, gives advice and instruction to help the penitent conduct himself better in the future. The counsellor, despite the name, gives no advice. He relies on the ability of his client to make his own decisions once he has become aware of the previously unconsciousness motives working in him. The aim of counselling is to strengthen the client's capacity to make decisions and this is weakened by giving advice. It assumes superiority, if not authority, in moral stature and in knowledge on the part of the counsellor and becomes a hindrance to the client's growth.

The confessor gives overt assurance of forgiveness to the penitent for his misdeeds and sinful attitudes. The counsellor gives no such assurance on behalf of God or the Church, but he *lives* forgiveness by the way he accepts his client as he is and passes no moral judgment on him. The confessor has the double aim of sharpening the penitent's understanding of his moral lapses so that he may condemn himself, and of convincing him that by rejection of this sinful part of himself he is received back into fellowship with God. The counsellor seeks to achieve recognition on the part of the client of what he is, but instead of rejection he wants the client to identify himself with this part of himself that he has judged to be bad so that it can be transformed positively into something good. By his own acted out acceptance of it in the client he transmits to him the experience of being forgiven while he is still (in his own opinion) bad.

These are important differences. The enumeration of them should be sufficient to dispel the confusion which results from the belief held by some that confession is a superior or inferior form of counselling. They serve different functions. It has sometimes proved valuable for the client to use confession during or after a period of counselling, or to follow confession with treatment by a counsellor. But it is not so clear whether the minister can be both confessor and counsellor (in the special sense in which the term is here used) to the same person. Some men have seemed able to combine the two roles, but it seems to require special gifts. Some clients seem to need both, but in their case the risk is run of using the formal confession as a therapeutic measure, using God as a medicine, and this has serious dangers. On the whole it is advisable for the pastor not to attempt to be both confessor and counsellor to the same person, even if as counsellor he probably hears a much fuller confession from his client than he would as confessor. As counsellor he should rely on the methods of counselling. We saw earlier that he must not try to be a psychotherapist, though what he does with his client will be therapeutic. In the same way he should not regard himself as a confessor, though he will hear all the secrets of his client. We might add here, to be expanded more fully in the next chapter, that he must not be an evangelist, though his work has a religious aim.

Let us then try to draw together the principles of pastoral care/counselling so that we can see wherein lies its distinctiveness when compared with related kinds of work. We have just been analysing the differences between confession and counselling, the chief being that confession involves a judgmental attitude which is totally absent in counselling. The specialist counsellor differs from the ordinary pastoral counsellor in that the latter must work from within the context of his normal parish duties, whereas the specialist is abstracted from them and, if he is sufficiently trained, may use some of the methods of the psychotherapist. The psychotherapist usually employs methods of interpretation of symptoms, dreams, etc., whereas the pastoral care/counsellor ought not to attempt these. There is another difference of considerable importance between the psychotherapist and the pastoral counsellor which may create difficulties for the latter and which demands training for it as rigorous as that which the former must undergo for his special skills. The psychotherapist is not necessarily a religious person. Many psychotherapists are and reveal it by their lives and by their interpretation of the work they do with their patients, but it is not an essential part of their training. On the other hand all pastors, and confessors, are essentially religious people and their profession is to foster religious beliefs and attitudes in their people. The psychotherapist aims to restore his patients to mental health. Only those of them who are deeply religious believe that this requires acceptance by the patient of religion and many who are themselves religious believe that this is a personal affair and make no effort to persuade their patients of its importance. The pastor must identify mental health with a religious way of life. Of course with any given client he may be content with lesser standards of mental health, but his temptation will always be to urge religion upon his clients. Certainly he will hope that what he does with them will lead them to belief. His eagerness for this may cause him to depart from the sound principles of pastoral counselling. He will always have a religious aim in his work, so he needs the rigorous training referred to above to enable him to integrate counselling and evangelism. We shall discuss this integration in the final chapter. If for the moment we may take it for granted that the religious aim of pastoral counselling is implicit and not explicit we may sum up the general principles governing it under four heads.

1. There is no effort made to directly manipulate the client, whether of a psychological, moral, or religious kind. Information, if asked for, may be given, and, on very rare occasions only, advice may be offered, not authoritatively but as an expression of the pastor's opinion to help the client in his own thinking. He must also be left to make his own decisions and be supported in them.

2. The pastoral counsellor will see his function as that of supplying to his client the love and understanding for lack of which he failed to develop maturely in the first place. Since mal-development is the result of failure in personal relations in the early childhood of the client, the pastor will establish with him a personal relationship in which he contributes the missing elements needed by the client. These are love and understanding, referred to just now, trust and full acceptance of him, whatever he is.

3. The relationship will be "client-centred", that is, it will be occupied in enabling the client to find himself. The needs and motives of the pastor should be kept in the background. This may appear to make the relationship one-sided, but this is the special nature of the counselling situation because the client came seeking help for himself in the first place and because his need by its very nature will keep it in the

forefront until it is settled. After that a normal two-way personal relationship may develop, but this differs from the counselling relationship.

4. The pastor must have faith that in helping his client to find himself, to become aware of his own motives and enabled to make his own decisions, he is doing what is best for him judged by *any* standard. He must desire this even if following his work with him he sees the client making what the pastor thinks are wrong moral decisions or failing to accept a religious way of life. This means that the pastor must believe that God values the freedom of persons more than their conformity with any pre-conceived ideal system of behaviour. It also involves faith in the innate desire for goodness on the part of all men, that given freedom from their own conflicts men will struggle towards the good, that God works from within all men as well as from outside them. Putting this in purely psychological terms, the pastoral counsellor sees his function as being to stimulate and foster the client's innate healing force, his urge to fullness of life. And he also accepts that the essence of religion is to bring fullness of life, life abundant (John 10. 10).

10

The Religious Aspect of Pastoral Counselling

The point made at the end of the last chapter brings to a head a difficulty that has been raised at various points throughout this book, namely, the relation of pastoral counselling to the full vocation of the parish priest and its place in religion. The basic question which has to be faced, and if possible answered, is whether a sound theological training is sufficient for the ordinary non-specialist pastor or whether he needs as well the psychological training without which he cannot be a good pastoral counsellor. I am leaving out of account the very few who by reason of special natural gifts and upbringing develop a skill at counselling without the training that the overwhelming majority of counsellors need. The question is: is training in counselling an optional extra for pastors or should it be considered an essential part of training? And if it is regarded simply as an extra, useful but not necessary, can it be adequately integrated to the rest of a pastor's work? If it is regarded as essential, in what way is it a mode of religious action?

We have seen that the pastor may have been strongly influenced in the choice and exercise of his profession by strong unconscious motives which get their satisfaction in it, in which case the genuineness of his religious attitudes is suspect. We may put these cases aside (though taking note that to some degree unconscious motives will be present in every pastor) and consider only the problems which issue from the acceptance of a sincerely religious vocation along with an appreciation of the value of the use of psychological methods in pastoral counselling. The two obvious problems, to which attention has already been drawn, but which now need to be examined more thoroughly, are, first, the conflict between the authoritative and authoritarian conception of the priest's office and the non-authoritative approach in pastoral counselling, and, second, the religious or directive aim in general ministerial work and the non-directive or client-centred methods adopted by the majority of pastoral counsellors. There is considerable overlap and interrelation in these two problems but we can look at them separately.

"Authority" is a word with many shades of meaning and it is easy to slip from one to the other unwittingly. For our purposes here there are four relevant uses of the term. First there is the legal or quasi-legal meaning, referring to rights and powers conferred on a person by reason of the office he holds. The minister is an authority because he has been duly appointed to carry out certain duties. The authority he wields attaches to his office and what it represents, rather than to his person. Secondly, there is moral authority, which depends partly on the office held by the minister and partly on the readiness of other people to accept the claim made for or by him that he represents God or the Church in his pronouncements. Legal authority is valid against all men but moral authority depends on its voluntary recognition. Thirdly there is the authority which comes from accumulated experience and knowledge. A man may be an "authority" on old silver, on modern painting, on lichens, on the Bible, on nuclear physics, because he has an extensive knowledge on these matters and his judgments about them are recognized as sound by other learned people in the same field. The authority he exercises depends on this recognition. In actual fact a man may be an "authority" on a given subject but have little influence on his fellows because they do not recognize the fact and pay no heed to his pronouncements. Fourthly, there is purely psychological authority in which a man may be esteemed, ostensibly on the grounds of the second and third types of authority, but derives his authoritative position from the emotional attitudes of those over whom he exercises it. The basic example of this is the authority a parent or other adult exercises over a young child. This fourth type becomes important because the infantile attitudes persist in the unconscious mind and lead us to ascribe authority to people where circumstances predispose us to it. This emotional authority, needless to say, because it is so largely unconscious reinforces or becomes confused with the other types.

The minister is an authority on all counts. About the first there is no question. His training and subsequent experience should give him the knowledge and wisdom to qualify him in the areas proper to his work on the third count. It is the second and fourth types of authority which raise special difficulties for him. If he adopts an authoritarian conception of religion and believes that it is his duty to bring all his parishioners to accept the doctrines he believes to be true and the standards of conduct which he holds as absolute or divinely ordained, then in all his work, counselling included, except for one possible outlet, he will be aiming to bring his clients to a similar acceptance, in which case he cannot be non-directive. We shall consider that point presently in the context of the second major problem. The possible outlet just now referred to is that he may regard his pastoral counselling as a work of charity, part of his ministry to the sick, and therefore calling for the suspension of his moral judgment. This means that he will use pastoral counselling entirely in a non-moral way, just as he might offer an aspirin to relieve a parishioner's headache, or try to comfort him when he has pneumonia or has broken his leg in an accident.

The parallel does not hold. In such cases of illness the pastor is not responsible for the medical treatment of the sick person, whereas in counselling cases he is deeply involved and can only be helpful because of the involvement. He becomes the healer. He is dealing with moral illness. He will be confronted with symptoms such as feelings of guilt, groundless fears and anxieties, depressions, compulsive drinking, quarrelsomeness, and so on, and he will have to listen to stories of marital infidelity, of sexual misdemeanours of every kind, of drunkenness, of hatreds and lusts, all of which reveal a parlous moral state in his client. Shot through it all will be irrationality, foolishness, and sheer stupidity. Can he avoid condemning such behaviour, and by doing so condemning the client also? If he holds the authoritarian concept of religion he cannot compromise with such behaviour. He must declare it to be wrong, that is, if he is to be consistent. This undermines his ability to be a good counsellor. He may be able to help his client to deal with this or that symptom by strengthening his controlling forces, the super-ego in particular, but he does not get to the heart of the illness. For that he must accept the client and his behaviour *as he is*. Unless he does so he cannot cure the illness, as we have seen. Because of this conflict between the authoritarian position in religion and the requirements of counselling, many faithful parish priests hold that they cannot be pastoral counsellors, for the attitudes they would have to adopt in counselling would contradict the rest of their work.

The effect on counselling of the authoritarian view of the parish priest's duties is most clearly seen when we look at it under the fourth heading, psychological authority. The client who is in need of help betrays by that fact that he is not fully mature, has not grown up and achieved inner integration. He carries infantile attitudes into his adult life. These predispose him to look for a parent substitute. The Church may be to him a mother figure, the minister will certainly be a father substitute. This is bound to happen at first whatever the attitude of the minister. The client coming to him sees him as an authority figure and the infantile in him responds accordingly. If the pastor sees himself as a moral and doctrinal authority, over and above his legal authority, he will inevitably confirm the client in the child-parent relationship. Since the value of counselling lies in stimulating the client to grow out of his childish fixations into maturity of outlook, the authoritarian position maintained by the pastor increases the difficulty of the client instead of helping him. The situation is not greatly improved if in his counselling work as pastor the minister tries to adopt a non-authoritarian attitude (as a methodological procedure) while retaining the authoritarian attitude in the rest of his work. If the client has dealings with him apart from the counselling sessions he may be split in a schizophrenic fashion from trying to adopt two different attitudes to the same man simultaneously, or he may lean on the authoritarianism to escape facing up to his unconscious motives, or he may be led to believe that the minister is insincere in one or other of his contradictory attitudes, and if in one then in both. As a consequence the client's chances of recovery can be greatly lessened. It would therefore seem inadvisable for a minister who holds firm authoritarian views to undertake counselling.

It may be thought that I am taking too narrow a view of authoritarianism in tying it to insistence on the acceptance of doctrinal and moral statements or principles, that it can value persons above systems of belief and practice and that the latter are only inculcated for the sake of the persons. This is confused thinking. One may believe that to be fully a person requires belief in God as he is described in certain dogmas, and with the belief standards that are prescribed by it, but to hold that belief and those standards does not make a man a unified person. A man only becomes a person by the exercise of freedom of choice, even though that opens the way to wrong choices. To exercise any form of constraint, whether mental, moral, or physical, is to place limitations upon that freedom and defeats the attainment of full personality. It is true that freedom is not absolute and has to be acquired in growth through the proper integration of all the functions of the mind, but this is only fostered by the continual use of what freedom has already been attained. If the beliefs we accept as absolute are true and the moral standards the highest, they will come as the result of full personal growth and any effort to impose them before that has been reached will defeat the end. And if full personal growth is attained, there is no need to inculcate them.

What has just been said also answers the question of whether counselling should be non-directive or have a religious aim. The pastor has an overall religious aim; he takes up counselling as a means of furthering this aim with his people. His immediate motive may be to express his own sense of charity by helping the needy and healing the sick, but if he is a good pastor and believes in his own religious ideas and values he will desire his clients also to grow into similar faith. This, however, must not be an immediate aim. He needs to believe that simply by helping his clients to overcome their difficulties and grow up he is freeing them to become religious or, if they were in some measure religious before, to deepen their religion and make it more mature and less infantile; to free it from the dominance of unconscious motives.

This question of an overall religious aim differs from the technical problem, discussed in an earlier chapter, of the use of directive or non-directive methods. When a lay counsellor or psychotherapist encounters his client the latter may be interested in what the former believes in, but at first it seems relatively unimportant and may, indeed, never be raised at all in the course of the treatment. But the pastor's client assumes from the beginning that the pastor has a religious outlook and aim, however badly he may misinterpret them. He will tend to expect to find this expressed in the pastor's relations with him. This places on the pastor the technical difficulty of assuring the client of his acceptance of him as he is. On the other hand most people have a deepseated longing, frequently largely unconscious, to reach a religious view of life, and this makes them more ready to seek help from the pastor. Over and over again the pastor will have clients who "feel sad" because they have lost their faith, or the power to pray, and others who long to have a faith but cannot reach one. These are the clients who are aware of their need, but many others are unconscious of what is really troubling them. The pastor cannot impose that faith from outside, he can only assist it to grow from within.

The client finds himself and grows through the living relationship set up between him and the pastor. To be a successful pastor requires complete reconciliation between his counselling work and the rest of his duties, and it demands that his counselling springs out of his religious faith and is an expression of it. This means, we have seen, that persons must be valued before systems of belief and morals. But it also implies that in his other, non-counselling, work the methods he uses and the attitudes he adopts must be at least non-contradictory to those which have been proved most successful in counselling, and probably they should conform to them. His preaching, for instance, ought not to be dogmatic but encouraging dialogue and discussion; his moral teaching pointing to ideals of conduct and explaining the reasonable justification of principles, rather than laying down laws. He will not condemn sinners but seek to understand their motives and to help them.

This may seem to be putting the cart before the horse, modelling the work of the minister on the methods of pastoral counselling instead of the other way round. But it is not so. The use of pastoral counselling has been attended with results which force a reconsideration of all aspects of ministerial work so that when unification of methods has to be sought it is counselling which becomes the model for the whole. It has provided a means of helping many in need who were previously beyond help and so enabled pastors to fulfil their responsibility to heal the sick on a scale not known before. It has opened the way to the understanding of "sinners" and made it possible to forgive and heal them. It has thrown new light on the nature of personality and made relations between persons the essential area of religious life, and has exalted love above virtue, lifting it from being a duty to being the expression of life freed within the individual. It has brought many to a deeper understanding of and faith in God. But above all it has given a glimpse of how God works and has enriched our understanding of his self-revelation. We have always known that theology, whether it be dogmatic, moral, or any other kind, is secondary to religion, derived from it and a rational interpretation of it, necessary because man's greatest ability is his power to reason and his thinking is a large element in his living. Moreover, thinking enables him to live and grow, so it serves to direct his growth. But in practice we tend to forget that ideas are secondary, so we are content to teach *about* religion and believe that in doing so we are teaching or imparting religion. We treat the Bible, and particularly the Gospels, as if God's primary purpose was to send teachers into the world to instruct us in knowledge about him, about the world and the hereafter, and to lay down principles to guide our conduct. We make Jesus into a teacher, a prophet, a law-giver, or even into a spiritual conjuror who is able to deceive both God the Father and the devil about the true state of men, and we overlook what was his chief work, namely, to live the divine life, and therefore the fully human life, as a man amongst men. Through association with him and by personal relationship with him this divine life was passed on and remains an element in the stream of events because men have grown in varying measures like him.

To enlarge on this would take another volume, or many volumes. All I need say here is that the practice of pastoral counselling has shown us how divided and despairing men may be made whole and that this is not the work of God from outside, it is God living in both pastor and client.

Suggestions for Further Reading

FOR PASTORAL CARE AND COUNSELLING

G. Bergsten, *Pastoral Psychology* (Allen & Unwin).

F. P. Biestek, S. J., *The Casework Relationship* (Allen & Unwin).

E. Bruder, *Ministering to Deeply Troubled People* (Fortress Press, Philadelphia).

S. H. Foulkes, *Therapeutic Group Analysis* (Allen & Unwin).

A. Godin, S. J., *The Pastor as Counsellor* (Holt, Rinehart, & Winston).

H. Guntrip, *Mental Pain and The Cure of Souls* (Independent Press, London).

Healing the Sick Mind (Allen & Unwin).

P. Halmos, *The Faith of the Counsellors* (Constable).

E. Heimler, *Mental Illness and Social Work* (Penguin Books).

J. S. Heywood, *Casework and Pastoral Care* (S.P.C.K.).

S. Hiltner, *Pastoral Counselling* (Abingdon Press, N.Y.).

D. Hooper & S. Roberts, *Disordered Lives* (Longmans Green & Co.).

F. A. Macnab, *Estrangement and Relationship* (Tavistock Publications).

D. Martin, *Adventure in Psychiatry* (Faber & Faber).

L. E. Moser, *Counselling, A Modern Emphasis in Religion* (Prentice Hall).

C. Rogers, *Counselling and Psychotherapy* (Houghton Miflin Co.)
Client-Centered Therapy (Houghton Miflin Co.).

D. W. Winnicott, *The Child, the Family and the Outside World* (Penguin Books).

The Maturational Processes and the Facilitating Environment (Hogarth Press).

FOR MORE GENERAL READING

G. Allport, *The Individual and His Religion* (Constable).

J. M. Argyle, *Religious Behaviour* (Routledge & Kegan Paul).

E. Biddle, *The Integration of Religion and Psychiatry* (Macmillan, N.Y.).

F. Braceland & M. Stock, O.P., *Modern Psychiatry* (Image Books, Doubleday).

J. A. C. Brown, *Freud and the Post-Freudians* (Penguin Books).

N. Brown, *Life Against Death* (Routledge & Kegan Paul).

Anna Freud, *The Ego and the Mechanisms of Defence* (Hogarth Press).
   Normality and Pathology in Childhood (Hogarth Press).
S. Freud, *The Ego and the Id* (Hogarth Press).
   Group Psychology and the Analysis of the Ego (Hogarth Press).
   The Future of an Illusion (Hogarth Press).
   An Outline of Psychoanalysis (Hogarth Press).
   Civilization and its Discontents (Hogarth Press).
   Inhibitions, Symptoms and Anxiety (Hogarth Press).
E. Fromm, *Psychoanalysis and Religion*
L. W. Grensted, *Psychology and God* (Longmans, Green & Co.).
   The Psychology of Religion (O.U.P.).
J. Hanaghan, *Freud and Jesus* (Runa Press, Dublin).
W. James, *Varieties of Religious Experience* (Longmans, Green & Co.).
R. S. Lee, *Freud and Christianity* (Penguin Books).
   Psychology and Worship (S.C.M.).
   Your Growing Child and Religion (Penguin Books).
V. Madge, *Children in Search of Meaning* (S.C.M.).
J. Nuttin, *Psychoanalysis and Personality* (Sheed & Ward).
A. Outler, *Psychotherapy and the Christian Message* (Harper).
D. Stafford-Clark, *Psychiatry Today* (Penguin Books).
   What Freud Really Said (Penguin Books).
Orlo Strunk, Jr., *Mature Religion* (Abingdon Press, N.Y.).
P. Tillich, *The Courage to Be* (Nisbet).
   The New Being (S.C.M.).
P. Tournier, *The Meaning of Persons* (S.C.M.).
   The Strong and the Weak (S.C.M.).
V. White, O.P., *Soul and Psyche* (Collins).
H. Williams, *The True Wilderness* (Constable).
D. W. Winnicott, *The Family and Individual Development* (Tavistock
   Publications).
   The Maturational Processes and the Facilitating Environment (Hogarth
   Press).
G. Zilboorg, *Psychoanalysis and Religion* (Gollancz).

Index